PRAISE FOR *LEARNING HABITS*

T0293761

Companies are competing at the pace of learning. *Learning Habits* is an actionable guide from an expert with more than 25 years of experience working with the world's top brands. A must read for any organization looking to drive business forward.
Mariangel Babbel, Director, Brand Marketing at Rev

Learning Habits is a great read that is based on sound principles, experience and solid research. I believe that it's a book with no time limit and a mandatory read to use as a reference tool within our field of workforce learning.
Julia Suk, Senior Vice President Enterprise Sales, hurixdigital|KITABOO, North America

Sarah Nicholl is a highly credible thought leader and practitioner in organisational change, and this book is jam packed with practised, repeated and proven steps and processes. I've witnessed the impact of what's shared in this book. Consider this a timeless roadmap for top executives, leaders/managers, and individual contributors.
Wendy Nagy, VP, Customer Success, Pluralsight

An invaluable guide for Learning and Development practitioners who want to build a learning culture in their organizations. Anchored around the famous habit cycle (cue, routine and reward), the book is packed with valuable practical examples and tips on building learning habits at individual, team and organization levels. It is a must-read for corporate learning professionals aspiring and experienced, searching for frameworks and tools to build a more holistic approach to learning ...Read this book - and learn from a true learning practitioner!
Pratima Krishnan, learning & organizational development practitioner and Chief Learning Officer, Techcombank, Vietnam

Want to build a world-class learning culture? Start here. You'll find an ideal guide to the latest research and best practices in organizational learning and performance. But you need more than theory - you need to put it into practice. That's where Sarah draws on her extensive experience to provide a practical roadmap: from meetings, reviews, the right goals and habits, to the right metrics to measure, and executive buy-in: everything you need to succeed.

Simon Allardice, Creative Director & Principal Author, Pluralsight

Learning must be an everyday reality for organizations and employees. Sarah's book, *Learning Habits* has a powerful message, approach and strategy for creating and supporting learning habits in these changing and challenging times. A must read!

Elliott Masie, Chair, The Learning Collaborative, USA

Written by a practitioner with clear focus on how to achieve learning habits, this is a well written, engaging book. It makes so much sense, it is a real page turner. The author is right on the money with her assessment of where business is at right now, and where it needs to head!

This is the first book I have seen to honestly outline why people like face-to-face courses. We were prepared to put up with online courses during the pandemic but now we are wondering where the benefits of face-to-face are hiding.

This book offers hugely useful mnemonics of AUTOMATIC and LEARN which help the application of a variety of ideas around forming and sustaining habits. LEARN offers a progress map for developing learning habits over time. Table 1.1 illustrates reality, and there are worked examples at every stage which help people to see themselves in the mnemonics and ideas. This is an important book for any L&D practitioner, OD practitioner, change manager, process consultant or senior leader in business. This book outlines strong arguments for why learning habits create successful businesses, and how you can engender such habits in your organization. A must read!

Michelle Parry-Slater, Director, Kairos Modern Learning, UK

This comprehensive guide is packed with practical tips and techniques to help you master critical learning skills. In today's rapidly changing world, learning is the key to success for individuals, teams, and organizations. Sarah Nicholl has done an outstanding job of compiling best practices into a detailed and well-researched resource for anyone responsible for learning. *Learning Habits* is a corporate learner's manual that provides actionable plans for anyone looking to incorporate the art of learning into their daily routine and foster a culture of learning around them. Whether you're a seasoned professional or just starting, this book is packed with relevant resources. Get a copy and take your learning skills to the next level!

Kevin Mulcahy, co-author, *The Future Workplace Experience*

Learning Habits

Drive a learning culture to
improve employee and business performance

Sarah Nicholl

KoganPage

Publisher's note

Every possible effort has been made to ensure that the information contained in this book is accurate at the time of going to press, and the publishers and author cannot accept responsibility for any errors or omissions, however caused. No responsibility for loss or damage occasioned to any person acting, or refraining from action, as a result of the material in this publication can be accepted by the editor, the publisher or the author.

First published in Great Britain and the United States in 2023 by Kogan Page Limited

2nd Floor, 45 Gee Street	8 W 38th Street, Suite 902	4737/23 Ansari Road
London	New York, NY 10018	Daryaganj
EC1V 3RS	USA	New Delhi 110002
United Kingdom		India

www.koganpage.com

© Sarah Nicholl, 2023

The right of Sarah Nicholl to be identified as the author of this work has been asserted by her in accordance with the Copyright, Designs and Patents Act 1988.

ISBNs

Hardback   978 1 3986 0914 3
Paperback   978 1 3986 0912 9
Ebook   978 1 3986 0913 6

British Library Cataloguing-in-Publication Data

A CIP record for this book is available from the British Library.

Library of Congress Control Number

2023930494

Typeset by Integra Software Services, Pondicherry
Print production managed by Jellyfish
Printed and bound by CPI Group (UK) Ltd, Croydon, CR0 4YY

CONTENTS

ACKNOWLEDGEMENTS

Writing a book is a large endeavour and it wouldn't have happened without a lot of support from my family, friends and colleagues.

This book wouldn't have been possible without the many amazing clients I've worked with over the years and many colleagues at learning companies. I've had mentors encourage me to write and colleagues helped me to connect with publishers. Kogan Page has been so supportive during the process, thank you especially to my editors.

I've worked with some amazing customer success consultants, past and present, in the learning industry who daily strive to support their clients and teams in using learning and with whom I have chatted, collaborated and shared ideas – thank you all. I've collaborated on account teams and with management which has made me think more clearly and see things differently – thank you. To those who gave their time for interviews, thank you so much.

So many friends have been cheerleaders through this whole process, I appreciate you all.

Mary, Jessica, Thomas, and Dad - thank you for listening about the book, for supporting the time needed and always being a cheering section as I worked through this project. And to my mom who passed away in 2019, I know she would have been happy to see her daughter publish a book, and it wouldn't have happened without her support and encouragement over all the years.

Finally, my husband and my boys. You are my constant cheering section, as I read new material and share ideas at the dinner table. My boys, Luke and Connor, who cheer me on and ask about my progress, helping me to get more done than I ever thought I would. My husband Raul who does so much to care for us and make it easy for me to have the time to research and write, and always encourages me to pursue my writing, I appreciate it more than words can say and I couldn't have written this book without you as my partner in life.

I hope others who are thinking about writing a book can read this section and be inspired that you can gather a cheering section to help you get there. We need to hear from more women so I encourage you to get your thoughts on paper and get them out into the world.

And finally, thank you for reading this book.

How to use this book

This book is structured in a very straightforward way that will allow you to gain an understanding of why habits are important, how they tie to learning and how you can build habits at the organizational, team and individual levels – for employees, managers and executives. You may have read other books about habits, and if so, you'll recognize some of the research references here.

I'll share a quick overview of each chapter and how to use each section depending on your role. The aim of this section is to give you an overview of the book so you can decide how to use it. You can then read the book all the way through sequentially or you can use this overview to determine which areas of the book you need to focus on. If you're looking to enable learning habits in your organization and want to share insights from this book, this overview will be helpful to guide you on which sections to share. You'll find a full description of the roles noted below and how they relate to learning habits in Chapter 20.

Part One: Getting started

1 **Introduction** – This chapter will introduce you to why learning habits are important in today's world. It will touch on digital transformation and the increased pace of change. It will then explain how these pressures make continuous learning imperative but hard to drive due to systematic challenges, and the context of moving from event-based to continuous learning. Next it will outline how this book will cover a model, approach and actional habits to drive learning in corporations.

TABLE 0.1 Introduction

Role/level		Use this section for ...
✓	Executive guidance	Big picture insight, purpose of the book and the perspective it is written from
✓	Programme management	
✓	Administration	
✓	Communications	
✓	Line of business executive	
✓	Manager	
✓	Individual contributor	

2 The need for a learning culture – This chapter reviews current definitions of learning culture citing popular works, and explains how organizations struggle with a definition of learning culture and therefore have trouble determining how to drive one. It will then explain why, based on digital transformation and the fourth industrial revolution, it is imperative to learn continually. Organizations can therefore look at what they repeatedly do in order to determine if they have a learning culture – we'll establish that learning habits can be used to define and measure a learning culture in an organization.

TABLE 0.2 The need for a learning culture

Role/level		Use this section to ...
✓	Executive guidance	Understand the why behind a learning culture and how learning habits fit
✓	Programme management	
	Administration	
✓	Communications	
	Line of business executive	
	Manager	
	Individual contributor	

3 Introduction to habits – This chapter highlights key concepts from popular works on habits and why habits are important – to give you an introduction if you're new to habits research and to give you context if you have read about habits before. It explains the anatomy of a habit – sharing a new diagram of a habit that combines approaches from across research.

Next, the chapter explains why this anatomy of a habit is particularly relevant to organizations as it includes context. It then explains how habits apply to learning; and how practitioners can view and map habits at the organizational, team and individual level. This tiered approach provides an actionable way to drive learning habits across levels within organizations. The chapter also covers how the habits outlined in the book are also in support of making learning stick, based on best practices from adult education research. The chapter explains the concept of a 'keystone habit' – how some habits cause a ripple effect and can lead to additional positive habits.

TABLE 0.3 Introduction to habits

Role/level		Use this section to ...
✓	Executive guidance	
✓	Programme management	
✓	Administration	
✓	Communications	Understand why habits are important and how they fit into learning
✓	Line of business executive	
✓	Manager	
✓	Individual contributor	

4 **Making habits AUTOMATIC** – This chapter focuses on behavioural science research in a way that practitioners can use in their organizational learning context. The chapter shares AUTOMATIC – a mnemonic that summarizes key insights from behavioural science to give practitioners a checklist to use people's thinking shortcuts and cognitive biases to nudge their organizations, teams and employees to stick with learning habits. Each letter of AUTOMATIC is explained with references to the supporting research, and the chapter outlines how AUTOMATIC will be used in each habit chapter to give the reader suggestions for how to make the habit AUTOMATIC in their organization.

TABLE 0.4 Making habits AUTOMATIC

Role/level		Use this section to ...
✓	Executive guidance	Learn how we can use our cognitive shortcuts to make habits stick for learning
✓	Programme management	
	Administration	
✓	Communications	
	Line of business executive	
✓	Manager	
✓	Individual contributor	

5 **The LEARN model** – This chapter puts the ideas of learning culture and learning habits together to outline the author's five level model to determine what level of learning culture your organization is at today and what level you may want to work towards. While models are by nature not comprehensive, the LEARN model provides a way to commonly talk about what learning culture looks like and by applying habits, how to move to a stronger learning culture. The LEARN model provides the framework and practical measurable reference that is missing within organizations today as they try to drive a learning culture.

TABLE 0.5 The LEARN model

Role/level		Use this section to ...
✓	Executive guidance	Understand how you can quantify a learning culture and where your organization is currently
✓	Programme management	
	Administration	
✓	Communications	
✓	Line of business executive	
	Manager	
	Individual contributor	

Habit chapters format

Specific habit chapters follow next. Each habit chapter is structured in the same format. It starts with a story; then gives an overview of the habit with a supporting graphic, then it shares suggested measurement for the habit and suggestions for how to make it AUTOMATIC, then a section for the reader to determine their action plan with the habit. Finally there is a wrap up of the story shared at the beginning of the chapter and an overview of key takeaways from the chapter.

Part Two: Organization habits

This section shares habits that can be used at the executive or organizational level to support learning across large divisions or company-wide.

6 Habit: AIM to LEARN – This chapter outlines a keystone habit that helps to drive learning throughout the organization (based on the LEARN model) in line with strategic priorities. It explains why this is a keystone habit; and shares an approach for how to use this habit with stakeholders. It does this by explaining AIM – which stands for Align, Improve, Measure to support moving further in a learning culture with the LEARN model.

TABLE 0.6 Habit: AIM to LEARN

Role/level		Use this section to ...
✓	Executive guidance	
✓	Programme management	
	Administration	Understand this habit and its application to align your organization priorities and habits annually
✓	Communications	
✓	Line of business executive	
	Manager	
	Individual contributor	

7 **Habit: Executive-led time for learning** – Following the habit chapter format, this chapter outlines this keystone habit – having dedicated time for learning for the organization, championed by executives, and how it helps to set the social norm and expectations for learning.

TABLE 0.7 Habit: Executive-led time for learning

Role/level		Use this section for …
✓	Executive guidance	
✓	Programme management	
✓	Administration	Establishing and driving dedicated time for learning across the organization and within a team
✓	Communications	
✓	Line of business executive	
✓	Manager	
✓	Individual contributor	

8 **Habit: Fiscal year start** – Following the habit chapter format, this chapter shares how to set expectations for learning in line with the fiscal year. It explains how executives can follow up at the beginning of the fiscal year to share expectations for their group and reinforce how learning supports the key performance indicators and results the group needs to achieve.

TABLE 0.8 Habit: Fiscal year start

Role/level		Use this section for …
✓	Executive guidance	
✓	Programme management	
	Administration	Establishing or refining a process to communicate expectations for learning annually
✓	Communications	
✓	Line of business executive	
	Manager	
	Individual contributor	

9 Habit: Company-wide meeting – Following the habit chapter format, this chapter shares how you can tie learning into company-wide meetings to support learning. It outlines how to include learning in the regular agenda to make it a habit.

TABLE 0.9 Habit: Company-wide meeting

Role/level		Use this section for ...
✓	Executive guidance	Establishing a routine for sharing learning through company-wide meetings
✓	Programme management	
	Administration	
✓	Communications	
✓	Line of business executive	
	Manager	
	Individual contributor	

10 Habit: Learning council – Following the habit chapter format, this chapter shares how to use a learning council to support learning in the organization. The learning council can be formal or less formal, and might have a different name (such as champion group), but it brings together representatives from across the business to share business insights and enable them to support learning in their respective groups.

TABLE 0.10 Habit: Learning council

Role/level		Use this section to ...
✓	Executive guidance	Determine if a learning council might work for your organization and how to establish or improve one
✓	Programme management	
	Administration	
✓	Communications	
✓	Line of business executive	
	Manager	
	Individual contributor	

Part Three: Team habits

After seeing the organizational level habits, the next grouping of habit chapters focus on team level habits. We know that teams are key influencers in groups using learning habits and this section shares habits that you may want to consider or refine to support teams.

11 **Habit: Quarterly business reviews and follow-ups** – Following the habit chapter format, this chapter shares how managers can follow up on their quarterly business reviews to support their team in learning during the quarter. The manager can reinforce how learning ties to the business results the group needs to achieve.

TABLE 0.11 Habit: Quarterly business reviews and follow-ups

Role/level		Use this section for …
✓	Executive guidance – support	
✓	Programme management – support	
✓	Administration – support	Guidance for managers on how to build learning into their quarterly alignment with the team
	Communications	
✓	Line of business executive – support	
✓	Manager	
	Individual contributor	

12 **Habit: Team meetings** – Following the habit chapter format, this chapter shares how managers can include learning prompts and discussions in their team meetings to support their team in learning regularly.

TABLE 0.12 Habit: Team meetings

Role/level		Use this section to …
✓	Executive guidance – support	
✓	Programme management – support	Understand how to integrate learning habits into your team meetings or how to support teams in integrating learning habits in meetings
✓	Administration – support	
✓	Communications – support	
✓	Line of business executive – support	

(continued)

TABLE 0.12 (Continued)

Role/level		Use this section to ...
✓	Manager	
	Individual contributor	

13 Habit: Manager one-on-one – Following the habit chapter format, this chapter shares how managers can include discussion points to support their direct reports in learning during their regular one-on-ones.

TABLE 0.13 Habit: Manager one-on-one

Role/level		Use this section to ...
✓	Executive guidance – support	
✓	Programme management – support	
	Administration	Understand how to integrate learning into one-on-ones or how to support managers throughout the organization using this habit
✓	Communications – support	
✓	Line of business executive	
✓	Manager	
✓	Individual contributor	

14 Habit: Performance review follow-ups – Following the habit chapter format, this chapter shares how managers can follow up on performance reviews with prompts to help their employees continue learning.

TABLE 0.14 Habit: Performance review follow-ups

Role/level		Use this section to ...
✓	Executive guidance – support	
✓	Program management – support	
	Administration	Consider how to adapt this habit for your team in line with your performance review process or how to support this across the organization
✓	Communications – support	
✓	Line of business executive	
✓	Manager	
	Individual contributor	

Part Four: Individual habits

This section shares habits that everyone as individuals can use to support their own learning in their own work.

15 **Habit: Log-on learning** – Following the habit chapter format, this chapter shares how individuals can tie learning to their existing cue of logging on in the morning and what their routine might look like.

TABLE 0.15 Habit: Log-on learning

Role/level		Use this section for …
✓	Executive guidance – support	
✓	Programme management – support	
✓	Administration – support	Everyone in an organization – this habit shares a way to tie to an existing cue to learn daily
✓	Communications – support	
✓	Line of business executive – support	
✓	Manager	
✓	Individual contributor	

16 **Habit: Follow-up actions** – Following the habit chapter format, this chapter explains how individuals can follow up on conversations with their managers to ensure they apply or build on their learning.

TABLE 0.16 Habit: Follow-up actions

Role/level		Use this section to …
✓	Executive guidance – support	
✓	Programme management – support	
✓	Administration – support	Understand how to follow up on learning with your manager to ensure you benefit from the learning
✓	Communications – support	
✓	Line of business executive – support	
✓	Manager	
✓	Individual contributor	

17 Habit: Collaboration channel – Following the habit chapter format, this chapter shares how individuals can use collaboration channels to deepen and embed their learning, while also increasing the social norm and visibility of learning on their team.

TABLE 0.17 Habit: Collaboration channel

Role/level		Use this section to …
✓	Executive guidance – support	
✓	Programme management – support	
✓	Administration – support	Understand how to use collaboration channels for your learning and help engage everyone in support of learning on the team
✓	Communications	
✓	Line of business executive	
✓	Manager	
✓	Individual contributor	

18 Habit: Accountability partner – Following the habit chapter format, this chapter shares how individuals can pair up with an accountability partner to support their mutual learning goals.

TABLE 0.18 Habit: Accountability partner

Role/level		Use this section to …
✓	Executive guidance – support	
✓	Programme management – support	
✓	Administration – support	See the value of accountability partners and determine if you want to use one yourself, or support others in doing so
✓	Communications – support	
✓	Line of business executive – support	
✓	Manager	
✓	Individual contributor	

19 Habit: Conversations – Following the habit chapter format, this chapter provides simple ways to tie learning into conversations at work or at home to help deepen and embed learning.

TABLE 0.19 Habit: Conversations

Role/level		Use this section to ...
✓	Executive guidance	
✓	Programme management	
✓	Administration	Determine if you are currently using this habit already, and if not, identify ideas you can apply to support your learning
✓	Communications	
✓	Line of business executive	
✓	Manager	
✓	Individual contributor	

Part Five: Bringing it all together

20 Bringing it all together – This chapter brings together the key points of the LEARN model, AUTOMATIC and habit highlights. It will share details of the roles involved in supporting learning habits and discuss alignment with your current set-up. It encourages the reader to use what they decided in reading the habit chapters, to move forward with the habits they want to build. It reminds readers that tying learning to existing habits makes it easier to move forward faster.

TABLE 0.20 Bringing it all together

Role/level		Use this section to ...
✓	Executive guidance	Determine how to combine the model and habits to create your plan for application
✓	Programme management	
✓	Administration	
✓	Communications	
✓	Line of business executive	
✓	Manager	
✓	Individual contributor	

21 Additional resources – This section shares resources to help assess and align the roles in your organization and explains materials that are available online to help the reader build learning habits in line with the LEARN model and make them AUTOMATIC.

TABLE 0.21 Additional resources

Role/level		Use this section to ...
✓	Executive guidance	Review the suggested resources and determine which ones you'll need or which ones your team could use
✓	Programme management	
✓	Administration	
✓	Communications	
✓	Line of business executive	
✓	Manager	
✓	Individual contributor	

As you can see, this is a very actionable book, written by a practitioner. You can read just the sections that you need, or read all of the book. You'll come away with a better understanding of the influence of habits in your organization and how to build learning into existing habits or foster new ones to help with learning.

Key takeaways

- This book has five sections – Getting started, Organizational habits, Team habits, Individual habits and Bringing it all together.

- It's recommended to read the introduction and then concentrate on the sections you need.

- Each habit chapter includes a story, details of the habit, suggestions to make the habit stick, measurement considerations and key takeaways summarized.

- There are stories that make the habits more real and actionable.

- By the end of the book, you'll have a plan you can use to drive habits in your organization, teams or for yourself.

PART ONE

Getting started

01

Introduction

Much of what we do every day is done out of habit. Look at your morning routine, for example – when you get up in the morning do you have the same sequence of events every day? Maybe it's get up, make your bed, shower, eat breakfast, start work. Or maybe it's get up, work out, shower, get kids ready for school, eat breakfast. You may even find that you eat the same thing for breakfast every day. All of this morning routine is done without really thinking about it consciously. This saves us time. If we had to decide and think through each choice we make every morning, it would slow us down and be very inefficient. It also takes up energy every time we need to make a decision – our brain is always looking to be more efficient and save energy, so we use habits to conserve our thinking power for when we need it (Duhigg, 2014).

We can harness this power of habits to help us. We know from many studies done that people who are more successful – those who are fit, have enough money and have strong support networks – they do not have more self-control than others, they simply have better systems and habits set up to support what they want to achieve (Wood, 2019).

In this book, we'll take the science of decision-making, research in habits and adult learning, and apply it to learning in organizations. We'll look at how what we know about how we think, our cognitive processes and biases, can be used to help us build learning habits across organizations, teams and individuals.

Why would we want to apply decision-making and habit research to learning across organizations, teams and people? Because embracing learning is hard. It forces us to admit that we need to change and grow. And we prefer the status quo – just like we use habits to be efficient in our morning routine – we want to continue on auto pilot wherever possible. So we put off learning, avoid thinking about how we can grow, and keep doing the same things we've done before. And let's face it, we are busy. We don't have time to change routine, examine what we're doing, learn new things and integrate them into our routine. We have bills to pay, we have results we need to get at work, we have families and social lives that need our time and attention.

But the world is forcing us to change this perspective. Without continuous learning, we will not be able to keep up, much less compete, in a world where profound uncertainty is the norm, not the exception (Harari, 2018).

An uncertain future

We like to think nostalgically about the past and how things were easier and less complicated in previous times. And some things were less complicated – while most of history was quite turbulent, we had an unprecedented period of peace and prosperity after the Second World War. That is changing now – the Great Recession propelled by the near collapse of our financial systems in 2007/08; the COVID pandemic with its public health restrictions in 2020 and the polarizing reactions to them in the two years since; volatile climate events and the growing effects of climate change; the rise of technology and the growth in artificial intelligence and machine learning, now the metaverse; technology's implications for jobs and life in the future – all of these things and more are pushing us to realize that we live in a world where change is constant, unpredictable and where we need to build our emotional and mental fortitude to survive. Learning habits can help us get there.

The approach in this book will break down the mysterious ways that we can build learning into our lives and our organizations. It is not complicated; it is repetition. After all, we are what we repeatedly do.

LEARNING IS LIKE EXERCISE

Learning is like exercise. You wouldn't expect to work hard to get fit, and then give up exercising and expect to stay fit – we know we have to keep at it to maintain fitness. Learning is a muscle that we need to maintain with regular, sustained use. But as organizations, teams and individuals, we have yet to embrace learning as a regular and sustained habit.

Shift in learning

There has been a major shift in corporate learning over the past 30 years, propelled even further by COVID and remote work. What shift am I talking about? The move from event-based learning to continuous learning.

FIGURE 1.1 Moving from event-based learning to continuous learning

We have shifted from event-driven learning that was face to face in a classroom to a continuous learning model with 24×7 access to learning resources. I'm not just referring to the abundance of learning materials available on YouTube or accessible from a Google search. In addition to those resources, corporations have moved a lot of their learning material online. They have set up learning management systems and/or learning experience platforms to enable access to learning materials they have purchased from learning providers and learning materials created within their organizations for knowledge transfer or compliance learning. Where before much of the learning done in organizations was done face to face in meeting rooms or corporate classrooms, or people were sent out to learning events provided by instructor-led training providers, now the focus has shifted to enabling continuous access to learning online.

This has made learning much more scalable. And with the uncertain future and need for learning across the enterprise, that is a very good thing – we need to scale learning to everyone. We know that really, classroom-based learning has a very important place in learning but is not scalable. It is expensive, hard to schedule and available to too few people. Organizations recognize this and spend money to buy learning systems with learning content aligned to their priorities.

But despite them having built it, companies struggle to get employees to use the learning assets. People like classroom training – they like that they get away from the office, their manager approves the time and cost of their course so they know the company values the learning, they get to chat with others about the learning and how it can apply to their work, they may even get other perks like free lunch and coffee and snacks. Outside of just the learning content, let's think about how event-based training supports learning in organizations.

With event-based learning:

- You get manager approval for the course.
- You know the company values the learning because they are paying for the course.
- You are given dedicated time away from your regular job to do the learning.
- You get a registration email, you get reminders, there is a penalty (usually) if you cancel at the last minute.
- You get to chat with other people in the class.
- You can discuss how to apply the learning in your work.
- You get lunch, snacks, coffee.
- You probably even get to wrap up and go home early on the days you're in the course.

These may seem like small things, but they add up to a major difference between classroom and continuous learning. In shifting from learning as an event, to learning as a continuous process, we need to recognize the differences and how they affect learners in their experience of learning within the organization.

Let's compare, generally speaking, how these factors differ between classroom and online learning:

TABLE 1.1 Shifting from event learning to continuous learning

Event learning (i.e. classroom, conferences)	Continuous learning (i.e. online, asynchronous assets)
You get manager approval for the course	Your manager may be unaware of what you are taking
You know the company values the learning because they are paying for the course for you	The company has paid for the learning, but not for you specifically
You are given dedicated time away from your regular job to do the learning	You have to fit the learning into your regular job and; when you learn at your desk, you will be (perhaps negatively) perceived as 'not working'
You get a registration email	You may have received an email when they launched the platform but nothing specifically for you now
You get reminders	You probably aren't getting any reminders
There is a penalty if you cancel at the last minute	There is no penalty for not learning, more likely you will be penalized for taking the time to learn
You get to chat with other people in the class	You do the learning alone and isolated
You can discuss how to apply the learning in your work	You have no immediate opportunities built into the experience to discuss to apply the learning in your work
You get lunch, snacks, coffee	You get what you usually have – no free lunch, snacks or coffee
You probably even get to wrap up early and go home early on the days you're in the course	You probably have to work late to make up the time that you spend in the online learning system or you do the learning on your own time

Employees are no longer given the time dedicated to learning, they are no longer assured of manager support for their learning, they are expected to fit in learning time within their regular job, and they are further expected to choose from a vast array of assets and pick the items that make sense for their role. Often, that is just too many decisions and too much friction to make it easy and appealing for people to learn online. In addition, they learn in isolation, they don't collaborate with others as they are learning, they don't have a free lunch or snacks, or get to go home early. These may seem like small things, but in a busy world, they can tip the scale to make learning online something the employee will put off to another day. These influences make continuous learning different, not just in the delivery mechanism of learning (online vs a facilitator in a classroom); it makes it a cultural shift that requires new ways of communicating, new ways of working and new habits for learners.

APPLYING THE LEARNING TO CHANGE BEHAVIOUR

Learning systems with learning content alone are not enough to drive learning and its application. If you've ever taken a course and thought, 'But that's not how we do that here' or 'This sounds good in theory but how am I going to use it?' then you know that learning material by itself is not enough to change behaviour and apply the new ideas and new ways of working. The application of the learning is part of the learning process and needs to be built into the learning habits as well.

The shift from event-based learning to continuous learning and the need to change behaviour to compete in a world of profound uncertainty is what we will address in this book through defining a learning culture by the habits people have, and then identifying the habits that we need in order to support the shift to continuous learning and its application in the workplace.

My experience of learning shifts

I've witnessed this shift in corporate learning first hand. As a young professional fresh out of school with a history degree but wondering how I would use that in a career, I started working at a stock brokerage firm after graduation in the early 1990s. I diligently took the Canadian Securities Course and struggled to grasp the concepts of analysing balance sheets and evaluating investments. When the firm started to roll out networked computers (yes, it was that long ago!) I applied to help train the stock brokers and assistants on how to use these new tools they had access to – MS Office and Windows, not to mention how to use a mouse. Most people at that time did not have computers at home so using the computer was not very familiar for them. One broker even held up the mouse and pointed it at the monitor like a TV remote, then wondered why it didn't work.

We rolled out computers to brokerage offices nationwide. I enjoyed the project and was excited to help people use the new technology in ways that made their work easier, and I continue to embrace that excitement about technology today. When the rollout ended, I moved into a newly formed computer education group, to help coordinate technical training across the investment bank.

I found adult learning so interesting that I went back to school to take a Bachelor of Adult Education focused on workplace learning. I learned the principles of andragogy – how adults learn – and what makes for effective learning design. At work, the department signed with a learning provider to provide computer-based training across the company. I was excited by this opportunity to help more people get access to technical training – to help them in their careers in information technology and to help them use the desktop applications that were becoming standard in the office. I could see that by putting the learning online – at that time it was on the Local Area Network and installed locally – it enabled many more people to get access to learning. No longer would they have to book five days off work and get approval from their manager not only for the time but for the substantial cost of the programme. But in that lay the problem – no longer would they get approval from their manager for the time to devote to learning and for the recognition of the value of the learning they were doing. So my job became to design ways to help people decide which courses they needed and to help them have the space and time for learning. I enjoyed the field so much I continued in school, part time while working, and did a Master of Education focused on learning work and change. I moved over to the provider side of learning so I could work for an organization focused on offering learning and enabling it in organizations. Since then, I have worked for four different learning providers in roles across customer success, marketing and professional services working with clients across the globe.

Through these roles, over the last 25 years in learning and development, I have worked with more than 200+ organizations globally to help them have successful learning programmes, including many from the Fortune 1000. I've worked with organizations across financial services, technology, telecommunications, retail, government and education in North America, Europe and Asia Pacific with companies ranging from one thousand to over two million employees. Since training those brokers on how to use their new desktop computers, I have focused my career on extending the reach of learning with technology.

With this in mind, I'm writing this book to share the approaches that I have seen work with telecommunications, financial services, retail, defence contractors, across large and small organizations in North America and beyond. While it is a very practical book, it isn't just a practitioner's approach – as I hope you can tell from my story so far, I am an avid learner myself. Since completing my graduate studies over 15 years ago I have continued to be a voracious reader so you'll see references to many books in behavioural science and psychology. I believe that not enough of us in corporate learning are applying what's been learned in the decision sciences to how people decide to learn in the corporate space.

The path forward

The need for effective learning has grown over the past 25 years and continues to expand. Now, more than ever, effective learning is important as we have to learn at a more rapid pace and we have to relearn continually. The pace of change is ever increasing. With the innovations in technology, we are in the midst of a 4th industrial revolution where companies are competing to innovate just to stay in business – the average age of the top 10 global companies has gone from over 57 years in 2010 to less than 34 years old in 2019. The proportion of tech companies in the top ten has grown as well (Lesser et al, 2019).

Companies are now competing at the rate of learning (Lesser et al, 2019). And many are struggling to do this. The COVID pandemic has brought to light the challenges many organizations face with rapid change and increased use of technology. And while the pandemic has increased the rate of change, even before the pandemic we recognized that the pace of change was already increasing and would strain our existing systems and attitudes. While we can't know the future for certain of course, it appears there is a very good chance that jobs are going to continually change, more than now, and there will be high numbers of low skill workers displaced resulting in high unemployment; and high vacancy rates in positions for skilled workers (Harari, 2018). All of this upheaval will cause stress. People will need even better coping skills and mental strength. The technological revolution will bring benefits but it will destroy existing jobs and with them identities, and it does this faster than people can shift to new jobs (Carney, 2021).

With this in mind, we can anticipate that the increasing use of technology, climate change and the expanding divide between haves and have nots, are going to cause massive upheaval. And what is the best way to protect ourselves and our organizations to be prepared to face this challenging and unknown future? By continually learning, by adapting and ensuring we are prepared mentally for what is coming. As you'll see in this book, I would argue the best way to do that is through building learning habits.

We know that when faced with uncertainty and anxiety about the future, one of the best coping mechanisms is action. The United Nations has helped the world to focus our action by framing the way forward with the Sustainable Development Goals. Learning is so important to sustainable development that the United Nations included a specific goal around ensuring inclusive and equitable education and lifelong learning (United Nations, n.d.).

We can focus our action on learning opportunities and ensuring we seek them out ourselves and support them in our organization. The Sustainable Development Goals are big lofty goals, but they are made real when we break them down into what we can do and how we can measure our progress. We can take what made classroom learning effective in the past, and integrate it into how we use a hybrid model of continuous learning to be prepared for the future. We can use learning habits to break down what we need to do and provide a way to measure our progress. We can start small and move forward – remember the saying – By the yard is hard but by the inch is a cinch. Start small and look for incremental improvement. We can make learning like our morning routine – automatic.

Making learning automatic

When we do actions through habit, they are automatic. And just like the successful people who have set up their habits so they don't need to rely on self-control to do the things they value, we can make learning habits automatic, and help our organizations support continuous learning. As we dive into the learning science and behavioural insight from research, we can see there is an abundance of evidence from behavioural science that points out why habits matter and how we can harness our own habits to change the culture and organization.

We often hear about the need for a learning culture, but like the sustainable development goal, it is challenging to achieve a learning culture if we don't break it down to a definition that makes sense and that has measurable ways to define what a learning culture is and what it looks like. We need to anchor on something to make it real. Everyone may have different ideas of what a learning culture is so we need a common frame of reference to be able to define and work towards.

To meet that need for a common reference, I'll share the LEARN model that will provide a measurable definition of a learning culture – using the habits across organizations, teams and individuals that make up the actions that constitute a learning culture. You will be able to see where your organization, your team and you, yourself are with habits, and determine where you want to get to. I'll share the AUTOMATIC approach to making habits stick – a mnemonic that combines insight from behavioural science research into a handy checklist that you can use to make habits work better. And then I'll share key organizational, team and individual habits that you can customize and use to build a learning culture in your organization or improve your own learning habits. Having worked with global organizations, I have seen first-hand how these habits can influence teams and organizations to build resilience and help prepare people for the future. It's a future that's only going to need more resilience and mental fortitude, making learning habits an integral capability we will all need to develop and improve.

Key takeaways

- We are faced with an uncertain future, driven by the change from technology innovations, increased inequality and climate change.
- As a global community, we have the sustainable development goal of inclusive and equitable education and lifelong learning opportunities – we need to make this achievable and scalable within organizations.
- Learning habits provide us with a way to prepare our organizations and ourselves for the future, and give us a measurable, incremental way to work towards supporting lifelong learning opportunities.

- This book will share practical ways to get started with learning habits, shared by a practitioner with over 25 years of experience, having worked with 300+ organizations globally.

- The LEARN model will be introduced and provides a way to measure where you and your organization are now, and give you a framework for where to aim towards in the future as you build a learning culture.

- The AUTOMATIC mnemonic will be introduced and gives you a quick summary of key insights from research in behavioural economics in a checklist format that you can use to make learning habits stick.

- Practical examples will be shared across learning habits for organizations, teams and individuals – all in a measurable way that will help you achieve results

References

Carney, M (2021) *Value(s): Building a better world for all*, Signal Penguin Random House Canada, Toronto

Duhigg, C (2014) *The Power of Habit: Why we do what we do in life and business*, Anchor Canada, Canada

Harari, Y N (2018) *21 Lessons for the 21st Century*, Penguin Random House, New York

Lesser, R, Reeves, M, Kimura, R and Whitaker, K (2019) Winning the '20s: A leadership agenda for the next decade. *Rotman Magazine*, Fall, 17–21

United Nations (n.d.) United Nations Sustainable Development Goals [online] sdgs.un.org/goals/goal4 (archived at https://perma.cc/Q4KB-SSMF)

Wood, W (2019) *Good Habits Bad Habits: The science of making positive habits that stick*, Farrar, Straus, Giroux, New York

02

The need for a learning culture

Sue Matthews* had worked at The ABC Bank for 15 years in various roles in the contact centre. The work was demanding and most of the time Sue found it somewhat tedious, but she needed the job and needed the pay cheque. She had two kids and appreciated the benefits from the company. She participated in the employee shareholder programme and owned some stocks in the company, which had been going steadily up. But over the last year or so the stock was underperforming the market. Sue didn't watch the stock price regularly as she had a lot to manage between work and family, but she did hear some rumblings about cutbacks at work.

The ABC Bank was focused on shareholder value, and when the stock was under-performing they looked to increase revenues or cut costs in order to drive more value and be seen favourably in the market. The bank was a global organization and their main region experiencing growth was Asia. With this in mind, the company looked to reduce expenditures in North America and drive more growth in Asia. This affected the contact centre where Sue Mathews worked. The company decided to shift resources to the lower cost labour market in Asia – not only would this reduce expenditures in North America where there was less growth, it would increase the bank's ability to better serve the Asia market where they were expanding and needed customer service representation. It would be a major shift for the customer service department and affect over 1000 jobs, but it was needed to drive shareholder value. Except driving shareholder value wasn't a reason that resonated with individuals like Sue.

When Sue Matthews showed up for work after the weekend she was not expecting to be called into a meeting with her manager. She had heard there was a town hall meeting but she hadn't received an invitation for that. Instead, when she went into the meeting with her manager, she was shocked to hear that her position had been eliminated and she was receiving a severance package. Her manager was obviously following a script and tried to reassure Sue, but as soon as Sue heard the news she thought to herself – what am I going to do now?

This story is typical of many organizations today, with departments across companies being affected by reorganizations that are designed to keep the company growing and maximizing shareholder value, but that leave individuals cast aside, needing to find new jobs elsewhere.

A learning culture can be a somewhat abstract idea and can seem like something that's a nice to have benefit, rather than essential to doing business. But the difference between having a learning culture and not having one can be dramatic and matters not just for the company as a whole, but for the individual employees as well. We'll return to Sue's story at the end of the chapter but rewritten with a learning culture at the organization. The difference is dramatic and matters more than we may think at first.

A focus on shareholder value

With the focus on shareholder value, companies are driven to put a value on everything and seek returns above all else. Prior to the 1970s companies saw themselves as responsible for a variety of stakeholders, including their employees. With the rise of shareholder capitalism and based on wide adoption of Milton Friedman's theory that the primary responsibility of companies is to drive profits, the landscape changed (Carney, 2021). We've seen unprecedented growth in the markets and an increased level of wealth for many but we've also seen rising inequality and greater disparity across wages (Harari, 2018). CEO's wages, compared to the average employee wage, have grown exponentially, even more so with CEO compensation being tied to stock prices (Rosenfeld, 2021). The wage disparity is so stark that some countries are looking to implement a cap on CEO compensation, as Emmanuel Macron indicated for France in the run up to his election in April 2022.

In addition to shareholder capitalism, the rise of globalization has also hit the average employee hard. With the drive to maximize value, companies seek to choose the geographies that will provide the best returns. This has shifted the job compositions in various geographies, at a rate that outpaces the individual's ability to change their skill set and identity (Carney, 2021). Many attribute this shift and the resulting impact on people's identities as one of the prime causes of rising populism, with people seeing wealth growing but not for themselves, and they don't see a path forward, so they long for a past when they perceived that jobs were more stable and provided better wages (Carney, 2021).

We have also added to this mix of change with the exponential growth in technology. Many jobs have already shifted, not by geography but by robotics. Manufacturing has optimized value by taking advantage of technology to reduce the number of workers needed to produce goods (Rosenfeld, 2021). We hear about the advancements in artificial intelligence and machine learning that will affect new categories of jobs. There have been shifts before, with the move from agrarian societies to manufacturing, with the invention of the steam engine powering a new shift in the world, and with the invention of the computer and the personal computer. We all know that the only constant is change, but that doesn't make it any easier to live with. With every phase of societal evolution, from the early industrial revolution to steam power to computers, society's jobs shift and people struggle to find a new place in a revised world.

The need for innovation

The average age of the top ten companies in the world is trending downwards quickly and trending towards tech giants (Lesser et al, 2019), meaning many companies are struggling to foster growth and stay relevant. In the race to provide shareholder value in a competitive landscape, companies need to innovate and they need to stay ahead of the competition. So perhaps focusing solely on immediate results for shareholder value is not the way to drive an innovative culture? If your people are focused singularly on the immediate results they need to deliver, they won't be able to learn and experiment, to provide the innovation you need for sustaining growth. And you don't know where the innovation will spark, it could be anywhere in the company, not just in the department designed for new ventures.

Companies like Amazon and Google know this and design it into their cultural context. Amazon is well known for their approach to pitching new business ideas. They require that the proposal is written on one to two pages, and no more than that (Carney, 2021). When they meet to discuss the proposal, the first 15 minutes is set aside for everyone to read the document. The next 15 minutes are for comments on the document. In this way, they have institutionalized clarity of thought through the need to write your proposal succinctly, they've institutionalized time to consider new ideas by putting aside 15 minutes in the meeting to read, and they've fostered collaboration and feedback in the meeting.

Google also builds time for experimentation and learning into their culture. They have established 20 per cent time for experimentation, learning and exploring new ideas. This built-in time for experimentation has helped drive much of the innovation at Google – including producing a way to capture street views too narrow for the google car with google tricycle and products like Gmail, developed during engineers' 20 per cent time (Schmidt and Rosenberg, 2017). Other companies have done similar structures for innovation – 3M had a 15 per cent time allocation for experimentation and learning – resulting in products like Post-It notes and Scotch tape (Schmidt and Rosenberg, 2017).

Verizon fosters a learning culture by showing support for learning from executives. When it's the annual learning days at Verizon, you'll see posts on LinkedIn from their CIO and other executives, sharing that they are having learning sessions.

Many other organizations aim to have a learning culture, but they aren't quite sure how to start or even agree on a definition of a learning culture. Let's turn to the definition now.

Learning culture vs learning organization

In *Harvard Business Review* (HBR), they define a learning culture as one characterized by innovation and experimentation (Groysberg et al, 2018). Creativity is fostered and leaders encourage exploration; curiosity is rampant. The focus is on experimentation and flexibility to follow one's curiosity; rather than a dedicated focus on results. According to HBR, the majority of organizations are results-focused with a sharp focus on measurable short-term results (Groysberg et al, 2018).

In Peter Senge's influential book, *The Fifth Discipline: The art and practice of a learning organization*, he outlines how a learning organization uses systems thinking, shared vision, team learning, personal mastery and mental models – together making the five disciplines, in order to define a learning organization (Senge, 2006). Each discipline supports how an organization can come together collectively to be a learning organization (Senge, 2006).

I propose that a learning culture can be developed to support an organization on the road to achieving learning organization status. In other words, we need a culture of learning to support innovation and experimentation, on the journey to being a learning organization. In order to have a culture of innovation and experimentation, people need the flexibility to be curious and to apply new thinking and new ideas in their work, they need to spend time learning and applying their new insights. We can define a learning culture by what people do.

> We are what we repeatedly do. Excellence, then, is not an act, but a habit.
> – attributed to Aristotle

With this in mind, I have built a definition of a learning culture that allows an organization to look at what they repeatedly do, in order to determine their level of learning culture now and where they would like to get to in the future. We can use learning habits to determine the level of a learning culture. A learning habit is a routine that supports learning triggered by a cue and followed by a reward, and occurring within a particular context. In other words, a learning habit is a recurring event that involves learning.

My definition of a learning culture is one where learning and experimentation is fostered and supported through habits that encourage learning and applying new skills and ways to work, at the organizational, team and individual level.

FIGURE 2.1 Definition of a learning culture

A learning culture is the measurement of how often learning habits occur (frequency), how much of the organization is using learning habits (ubiquity) and how many learning habits are occurring (depth).

Frequency (how often are learning habits occurring?)

Ubiquity (how much of the organization is using the learning habits?)

Depth (how many learning habits are occurring?)

= Learning culture

We can use learning habits, in a learning culture, to move towards the attainment of a learning organization. One way of thinking about this is that an organization may have informal and unarticulated conventions about learning. By articulating their learning habits and building the context of a learning culture, they can move to a stage that embeds learning in how the company does business. This can lead to being a learning organization across Senge's five disciplines. With the business context that we visited earlier in the chapter, we want to start on this journey of a learning culture.

THE NEED FOR A LEARNING CULTURE

We know organizations seek to maximize shareholder value. Shareholder value needs innovation to stay competitive. Innovation needs learning and experimentation to flourish. Learning needs to be part of the social norms of the organization in order to foster innovation and drive shareholder value.

- Companies need to drive shareholder value.
- Companies need to be competitive to drive shareholder value.
- To be competitive, companies need innovation and experimentation.
- To have innovation and experimentation, companies need people learning.
- To drive learning, companies need to establish social norms supporting learning.
- A learning culture supports social norms of learning in an organization.
- A learning culture drives shareholder value.

Organizations are made up of people. And people act out of habit for much of what they do. So if we want to change what people are doing, we need to look at the habits in the organization and foster habits at the organizational, team and individual level that will support learning and make it a social expectation within the company. By supporting learning, we can help people innovate and in turn create value for the organization but also make for better companies to work for, more enjoyable work and more fulfilling lives. With that, let's return to the story we started the chapter with – but let's rewrite her story in the context of a learning culture.

Back to our story

Sue Matthews worked for The ABC Bank. She has worked there for 15 years across various departments. Sue knows what the bank stands for and she is personally committed to the mission. The bank has been challenged with fostering growth in North America. Sue's team has proposed a new idea to launch an innovative product and

Sue is excited to get started. There is a town hall meeting coming up and Sue is going to share what her team has proposed and the timelines for launching. It's going to be a lot of work to create the new offering – financing for female-led businesses – but she's excited to get started. She met with her manager today, and they put the final touches on the town hall presentation. She and her manager were discussing that if it hadn't been for the learning and development that Sue and her team had been doing during the one day every two weeks for passion projects, they would never have uncovered this market need and developed the idea. Sue can't wait for the future. And as a shareholder, she's excited to see the market's reaction as more sustainable products that help the community are launched. The ABC Bank is fully committed to conscious capitalism and, as a mother of two children, Sue stands behind the idea of making the world a better place for the next generation.

While our story is a simplified one, the example shows that individuals and organizations can benefit when people are engaged, committed and aligned to drive results for themselves, their communities and their organizations. There are macroeconomic forces and global changes that are outside of our control, but we can look to what we repeatedly do, and the learning habits we're using, to make for more interesting work and better results, and together that makes a learning culture that benefits everyone.

Key takeaways

- The drive for shareholder value combined with globalization and changes in technology means that companies need to innovate to stay relevant.
- Innovation is the result of learning and experimentation.
- Companies need to move from informal conventions around learning to a rules-based architecture to embed learning in the fabric of the enterprise.

- By examining the habits of the organization, teams and individuals, learning can be embedded in how business is done.

Endnote

*This is a fictional story for illustrative purposes, based on several real life examples.

References

Carney, M (2021) *Value(s): Building a better world for all*, Signal, McClelland and Stewart, Toronto

Lesser, R, Reeves, M, Kimura, R and Whitaker, K (2019) Winning the '20s: A leadership agenda for the next decade. *Rotman Magazine*, Fall, 17–21

Rosenfeld, J (2021) *You're Paid What You're Worth and Other Myths of the Modern Economy*, The Belknap Press of Harvard University Press, Cambridge, MA

Schmid, E and Rosenberg, J (2017) *How Google Works*, Grand Central Publishing, New York

Senge, P (2006) *The Fifth Discipline: The art and practice of the learning organization*, Currency Doubleday, New York

03

Introduction to habits

A little while ago, a baker received an order for cupcakes for a party. They gathered their ingredients and baked the cupcakes. It was an order for a children's birthday party where some of the children attending had severe allergies. The baker was careful to make the batter without any egg, tree nuts, peanuts or dairy. They put each cupcake into its own container and labelled the box as containing no eggs, no dairy, no nuts. The order was all set for the party and the kids would be able to enjoy the cupcakes.

Except, out of habit, the baker had used royal icing. And their royal icing mix contained egg whites.

At the party, one of the children with allergies bit into a cupcake. Immediately he told his mom his tongue felt funny. This child had a life-threatening allergy to eggs. A few minutes after he took a bite from the cupcake, he vomited, his torso was covered with hives and, worse still, his throat started to close. The boy's father administered epinephrine with an auto injector and the mom called for an ambulance. With the medication, the anaphylactic reaction subsided. At the hospital, the boy was given steroids to ensure the swelling stayed down and that his airways stayed clear. He recovered fully from the reaction. In fact, a few years later he was teaching other kids about allergies and how to use an auto injector.

Habits can work against us and habits can work for us

This story illustrates how habits can work against us and how habits can help us. A habit is made up of a cue, routine and a reward. For the baker, the cue was the cupcake order for the party, the routine was to bake the cupcakes and put icing on them, and the reward was fulfilling the order and the kids having delicious cupcakes to enjoy. Many of our habits are done without us having to think about them – that's why they're valuable as they free up mental resources that can then be spent elsewhere. Except sometimes the context changes and we need to pay attention. If we don't, then mistakes can happen – like using the icing with egg whites when the order was for a party with kids with allergies.

Habits can also work for us – as with the family managing allergies. The cue for them was the evidence of a reaction. Their routine was to administer epinephrine and call for an ambulance. The reward was the reaction resolving and their son being healthy. And in this case, knowing the routine to follow when the reaction started helped them free up precious mental resources to stay calm and reassure their son that he'd be fine and that help was on the way. Habits can help us.

Habits research

There has been a lot written on habits – you may have read many of the popular books yourself such as *Atomic Habits* (Clear, 2018), *Tiny Habits* (Fogg, 2020), *Good Habits Bad Habits* (Wood, 2019) and *The Power of Habit* (Duhigg, 2012). There has been a lot of research on how we think, what mental shortcuts we use – books such as *Thinking Fast and Slow* (Kahneman, 2011) and *Influence* (Cialdini, 2021) are two standout titles among many others.

What we know from the research is that we use mental shortcuts to reduce how many decisions we have to make in a day. Many of our mental shortcuts are very helpful and allow us to free up resources to concentrate on other things. We use our mental shortcuts to go into automatic mode – and we form habits out of what we do regularly, to make it easy to follow. But sometimes our mental shortcuts are faulty and lead us to biased judgement or incorrect assumptions; and sometimes we act out of habit when we should be taking note of a change in context.

We act out of habit for more than 40 per cent of our day – our morning routine, our work routines, our evening routines, much of this is done the same way every day (Wood, 2019). Our routines can have a jolt if we move locations or change our situation – for example, when we're on vacation and staying in a new place we often switch up our routines. On a more global scale, the pandemic changed many people's routines and resulted in a lot of mental health challenges from the resulting strain. Our habits are very dependent on our context. When we change the context, it throws off our habits.

We know that habits are made up of a cue, routine and a reward, and they are context dependent. Viewing a habit in its parts can help you to understand what's happening and how to improve your habits. Let's break it down.

A habit starts off with a cue, something that triggers you to start the routine. For example, your alarm going off in the morning is a cue – it triggers you to get out of bed, make your bed and get in the shower. The routine is what you do after the cue – making your bed and getting in the shower. The reward could be having a tidy room, enjoying a hot shower or starting your day off on time. Rewards can be small things that make you feel good; they don't have to be large rewards. They can be as simple as smiling to yourself when something is accomplished or a fist pump in the air to celebrate (Fogg, 2020). Surrounding the cue, routine and reward is the context. This is the environment that the habit occurs in – it is the set of social norms and situations that affect your habit. For example, in your morning habit, if you're on vacation and not at home, the context changes so you may not have the same morning routine – you don't set an alarm, when you do wake up, you may not make the bed or get in the shower right away, your routine changes. The rewards on vacation are different as well; you may smile while walking on the beach in the morning, rather than enjoying a tidy room when your bed is made. The context of a habit, especially the social norms, matter a great deal when we start to look at team and organizational habits, but more on that later. First let's look at what makes up a habit.

Anatomy of a habit

We can put the components of a habit together in a graphic that can help us map out habits – here is the anatomy of a habit, with the cue, routine, reward and the context influencing the habit.

FIGURE 3.1 The anatomy of a habit

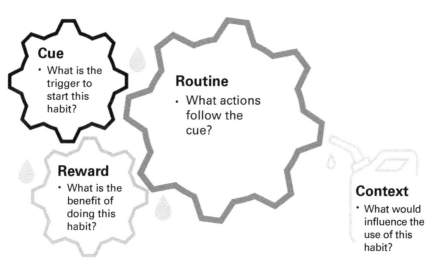

As shown in Figure 3.1, the habit starts with a cue, which triggers a routine, and then has a reward. The context for the habit is central to the habit and it also surrounds the habit. If we return to the cupcake example from the start of the chapter, here's how the baker's habit would break down:

FIGURE 3.2 Baking cupcakes habit

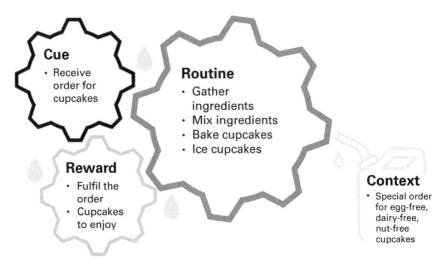

FIGURE 3.3 Handling a reaction habit

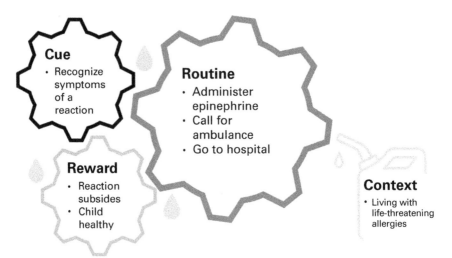

Similarly, we can map out the habit for handling a reaction (see Figure 3.3).

With the handling of the reaction example, we can see that this family has a routine for managing reactions, and this helps them to be able to concentrate on reassuring their child that everything will be okay. Their context is important – they are living with life-threatening allergies so they are vigilant about food and managing reactions quickly. If we change the context, and a reaction had happened for the first time, to a child with no known allergies, the family would have reacted quite differently. The context matters a great deal.

By mapping out habits this way we can make our habits visible and examine each component to optimize our habits. This works for our personal lives, our work lives and across the organizational, team and individual levels at work.

Habits are the way we live out our mental models. A mental model is our framework for viewing the world; it includes our assumptions about how things are and how they should be (Senge, 2006). As our mental models may be unexamined and unconsciously influencing how we see the world, we can examine them by looking at our habits and what assumptions are driving our habits. This is incredibly important as it is through our actions that we live our values and live our lives; if we set up our habits so that they drive actions in line with our value and goals, we can go back to being on autopilot but in a way that supports what we're trying to accomplish. In the absence of this habit set up, our habits can work against us and we are reliant on willpower and self-control to drive our actions towards where we want to go. We are creatures of habit so we generally don't do well if our context and our habits are not in support of our goals. As Wendy Wood found, people who are generally successful in accomplishing what they intend to do, do not have stronger willpower or self-control, instead they have optimized their habits to support the goals they want to achieve (Wood, 2019).

Habits in organizations

Habits apply to everything we do, and they apply to learning in organizations. As we'll see in this book, there are habits that can support learning in organizations. Organizations have habits. Teams have habits and individuals have habits.

FIGURE 3.4 Levels of habits

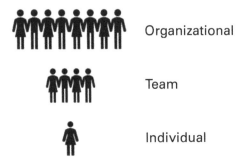

Organizational

Team

Individual

There are existing habits at all of these levels. For example, your organization most likely has a routine around annual planning. You may have regular company-wide meetings that occur annually or quarterly. The way that departments collaborate can also be a habit, with an existing cue, routine and reward.

At the team level, many teams have regular meetings, the manager may have regular one-on-ones with team members, and the work done by the team aligned to the key performance indicators (KPI) they are responsible for, can align to cues, routines and rewards.

At the individual level, people have their own work aligned to the key performance indicators, and they have their own daily routine for work habits and their own way of collaborating with others. There are many other habits across these levels, and the context at each level is different depending on which organization they occur within, which team and which individuals.

FIGURE 3.5 Levels of habits with examples

Organizational habits		Annual planning Company-wide meetings Cross-functional collaboration
Team habits		Team meetings Manager one-on-ones Work aligned to business results
Individual habits		Work aligned to individual targets Daily work habits Collaboration

These habits are ongoing at all these levels. We can infuse learning opportunities into these existing habits to take advantage of what people are already doing and shift the culture towards a learning culture. We are what we repeatedly do, and we improve in small increments. If we infuse learning into existing habits, we'll shift towards a learning culture.

Adult learning

Learning science and adult learning shows us that as adults we may be resistant to learning and we fear hurting our professional reputation by slowing down to try something new or experiment with a new behaviour (Brookfield, 1990). But it is within that experimentation that we learn. Adults struggle with thinking 'That's not how we do things here' or 'How would this work in real life?' How often have you thought this to yourself when in a class or learning something new? I remember thinking it quite often during math class in high school. But even in corporate learning, people need to have solid examples of how the idea applies to their own work, in their own context. Then they need time to apply the new idea or concept in their own work.

As Carol Harper, Director Leadership Learning and Development (retired) says, embracing learning needs to involve the head, heart and hands (Harper, 2022). For the head, you can explain new ideas, and share new concepts, but the only way to get people to adopt new behaviours is by getting to their heart and hands. We need to provide opportunities to practise new ways of doing things, try it out and get feedback. This will help people shift their thinking and adopt new behaviours as their own – with their heart and hands. It is by generative learning – actually trying things out, experimenting and creating, within the context of our work, that we learn and update our own mental models (Senge, 2006). By using the learning habits suggested in this book it will help to make the learning stick.

Adding to the need for habits, as we've discussed, the world is changing rapidly, and will continue to change, most likely at a progressively faster pace. This increase in technological change and its impact on society, will mean that we need to increase our mental fortitude in order to manage, much less succeed, in this changing world. And one very solid way to increase your mental fortitude, is to look at your habits and optimize them to make the behaviours that you need to succeed more automatic.

Research has shown that people who are healthier, wealthier and happier, aren't people with more self-control (Wood, 2019). Instead, they have set up the systems and habits to make it easier for themselves to follow the habits that make them successful, rather than relying on willpower, or actively deciding everyday what actions will bring them health, wealth and happiness. We can build a learning culture by setting up habits that integrate learning, instead of leaving learning to informal conventions and individual willpower.

Why are learning habits important for organizations, teams and individuals today?

Learning habits are important for organizations today because attention is scarce and time is always a constraint. There is pressure on organizations to innovate to stay competitive; and the move from event-based learning to continuous learning as discussed in Chapter 1 means there is no choice but for organizations to promote learning habits. The rapid pace of change and the increased need for mental fortitude to handle the pace of change will also make habits increasingly important.

Organizations that we once thought were stable and long term are no longer assured of their place in the market. We're all familiar with Blockbuster and their very public demise – they turned down a partnership with Netflix because they couldn't see the need to innovate beyond their currently successful business in renting DVDs (Hastings and Meyer, 2020). We're also familiar with the way that Facebook and Twitter try experiments to test new features – and the way Facebook watches the market for competitors with features they need – and often buys competitors to get the features they need, as they did with Instagram and WhatsApp. Publicly traded companies are only as good as their last results – or their current projected growth. We saw that with Netflix's drop in share price in April 2022 after announcing their subscriber loss and expected continued subscriber decline. Despite Netflix continuing to dominate the streaming market based on number of subscribers, when they could no longer project growth, markets reacted strongly and there was a sharp selloff of Netflix shares.

People in organizations are seen the same way. Organizations are increasingly expecting constant growth from their people, but the organization needs to be prepared to support their people with development tools and the time and social acceptance for learning. Fail fast and learn doesn't just apply to Silicon Valley start-ups anymore – it is becoming the way of working.

But organizations are often unconsciously operating in an instructor-led training mindset and many aren't yet supporting their people in building learning habits. By that I don't mean they shouldn't be doing instructor-led training – of course not – it's a good way to learn in a lot of cases and has a valid place in a corporate training strategy. Rather, what I mean is that organizations are providing development tools that are online and always accessible but they are missing the intangibles that come with event-based learning – demonstrated manager approval, time blocked for learning and executive support, as we discussed in Chapter 1. When you book an instructor-led class, your manager approves the class and the time to take it, you receive reminders for the class, there may even be penalties for cancelling late, you know you have executive support for the class because they approved the development dollars in the budget and the class conforms to the expectations of how those budget dollars should be spent. But when the company offers continuous learning, they may launch resources, let people know it's available and then leave it up to managers and employees to use the resources available, without realizing people will be missing the cues that come with instructor-led learning. With no reminders, no time blocked, no expectations set; the learning is left on the shelf. If you have a learning ecosystem with development offerings, encouraging learning in the organization needs to be an ongoing habit like exercise, not a set it and forget it approach. You wouldn't expect to stop exercising and still stay in shape, you need to do it continually to keep the health benefits. The same applies for learning; you need to keep learning habits ongoing to get the benefit of learning in the organization.

Keystone habit

A keystone habit is one that has a ripple effect across the organization or the person. It's a habit that sets off a chain reaction to improve other habits around it. Maybe you can think of a keystone habit in your life?

Let's return to exercise as an example again, as it's a keystone habit for many people. Once they get into the habit of exercising every day, they want to eat better as they don't want to ruin the good effects of their exercise. They are more active and feel better, so they may enjoy being with family and friends more than before. Exercise can trigger a virtuous cycle that can help them improve across many areas in their lives. It's a keystone habit that has a ripple effect across many areas of their lives.

Returning to our example of the family managing allergies – the need to manage food allergies can be a keystone habit for a family. They read the ingredients on everything they eat, they advocate for their child and the child learns to advocate for themselves – they can speak up and ask even someone in authority, what's in the food, and then not eat it if it isn't safe. Vacations can be quite different because they don't eat in restaurants – they book accommodation with a kitchen. The need to know what's in your food every time you eat is a keystone habit that has a ripple effect across how you shop, how you go on vacation, how you advocate for yourself and your level of comfort in speaking up to those in authority.

The idea of a keystone habit is not new – Charles Duhigg explained it beautifully in his book *The Power of Habit*. He shared the story of how Alcoa used safety as a keystone habit – by putting safety first, it caused the business to look at all processes and products through the lens of safety – it empowered employees to speak up if they saw something that needed changing. This led to new efficiencies and to new product ideas. The stock market responded and the company value increased. Safety was a keystone habit for Alcoa (Duhigg, 2012).

In learning habits, there are keystone habits too. These habits have a ripple effect and help support learning across many areas. When we dive into learning habits, we'll have a look at which organizational habits are keystone habits for learning. But first, let's dive a little deeper in those shortcuts in our thinking and how we can use them to make our habits automatic – in the next chapter.

Key takeaways

- A habit is made up of a cue, routine, reward and context.
- We can use the anatomy of a habit to examine our mental models and unconscious behaviours.
- Habits can work for us and habits can work against us.
- Habits occur at the individual, team and organizational levels.
- Keystone habits cause a ripple effect and help drive other habits.
- Habits can support learning in the organization, and many of the habits outlined in this book integrate ideas from learning science and adult learning to help make learning stick.

References

Brookfield, S D (1990) *The Skillful Teacher*, Jossey-Bass, San Francisco

Cialdini, R B (2021) *Influence: The psychology of persuasion*, Harper Business, New York

Clear, J (2018) *Atomic Habits: An easy and proven way to build good habits & break bad ones*, Avery, New York

Duhigg, C (2012) *The Power of Habit: Why we do what we do in life and business*, Anchor Canada, Toronto

Fogg, B (2020) *Tiny Habits: The small changes that change everything*, Houghton Mifflin Harcourt, Boston

Harper, C (2022) Director, Leadership, Learning and Development (retired) [Interview] (29 April 2022)

Hastings, R and Meyer, E (2020) *No Rules Rules: Netflix and the culture of reinvention*, Penguin Press, New York

Kahneman, D (2011) *Thinking Fast and Slow*, Anchor Canada, Toronto

Lesser, R, Reeves, M, Kimura, R and Whitaker, K (2019) Winning the '20s: A leadership agenda for the next decade. *Rotman Magazine*, Fall, 17–21

Senge, P (2006) *The Fifth Discipline: The art and practice of the learning organization*, Currency Doubleday, New York

Wood, W (2019) *Good Habits, Bad Habits: The science of making positive changes that stick*, Farrar, Straus and Giroux, New York

04

Making habits AUTOMATIC

Why do you think Instagram, Facebook and TikTok are so habit forming? What do these companies know about how we think to get us so hooked on using their platforms?

What all these companies have in common is a deep understanding of behavioural science and how our cognitive biases can be used to make us keep coming back for more. They hire behavioural scientists to design their products to optimize product stickiness based on research and the vast access to data that their platforms provide. A quick perusal of job postings across Meta, Google and TikTok shows job descriptions looking for people with research backgrounds in behavioural economics to inform product and marketing strategies, across multiple teams and geographies.

These companies also support research in partnerships with universities to drive further insight, often through a foundation arm. For example, in the funding notes for a research article titled 'Beyond Willpower: Strategies for Reducing Failures of Self Control' is the Chan Zuckerberg Foundation as a funding provider (Duckworth et al, 2018). That is the foundation of Priscilla Chan and Mark Zuckerberg of Facebook, now Meta. The article shares insight on how to reduce failures of self-control in areas like overeating, procrastination and more. The suggestions included can be used to support many behaviours – and they also provide insight that can be applied to design products that are more habit forming.

Many of the employees and executives of successful persuasive technology start-ups are graduates of prestigious universities who do research on behavioural science – for example, the author of *Tiny Habits*, B J Fogg, mentions that the founders of Instagram took his course on habits at Stanford and successfully applied the concepts to make Instagram appealing (Fogg, 2020). These tech companies use our mental shortcuts to make their products more engaging. They have extensive resources to hire, experiment and use the data from their platforms to ensure their platforms are habit-forming.

As Richard Thaler points out with his concept of libertarian paternalism, ethically speaking, we want to gently nudge people in a positive direction, not use their cognitive biases to trick them into doing things they don't want to do. Stanford University's Behavior Design Lab outlines the ethics involved in persuasive technology specifically on their website at https://behaviordesign.stanford.edu/ethical-use-persuasive-technology. The field of behavioural science is concerned with the ethical use of the insights from research – for example, the University of Pennsylvania has a research lab called the Behavior Change for Good Initiative.

We can confidently use behavioural science insights to drive learning in organizations as its use fits within the parameters of the ethical use of the insights and supports people in learning that helps them. However, most likely your organization does not have the funding to hire PhDs in the behavioural sciences to drive your learning initiatives. Even learning technology companies, themselves, often don't have behavioural scientists on staff. But there is a lot we can use from the research to support learning habits in our organizations, even without having PhDs on staff. And habits research shows, if we make it easy, we're more likely to use it.

This chapter has a summary of the research on the mental shortcuts we use, which I have built into a mnemonic – AUTOMATIC. Each letter of the mnemonic shares a key insight from the research that you can use to drive learning behaviour. We know from research in the field of cognitive poetics that items set to rhyme are more likely to be remembered and that they are seen as more valid (Cialdini,

2016). With this in mind, each letter of the AUTOMATIC mnemonic has a short rhyming phrase to make it easier to remember.

While the tips summarized here are focused on learning habits, the mental shortcuts they reference affect much of our behaviour in Western societies. There are cultural differences in our mental short-cuts, so keep in mind as you read this that the majority of research studies in behavioural science have been conducted in Western universities – specifically on WEIRD societies (Western, Educated, Industrialized, Rich, Democratic) (Henrich, 2020). As with all research, it's a good idea to view it with a critical lens and consider how it applies to the population we're working with, and where there may be exceptions or instances where it doesn't apply. In other words, the mnemonic is generally applicable, but you can apply it in ways that work for your particular audience.

AUTOMATIC: a mnemonic to help us drive our habits

Allow for feeling good

The first A in AUTOMATIC is 'Allow for feeling good'. What does this mean? It means that we do better when we enjoy things. We may know this intuitively but we often forget this when designing learning programmes in the workplace. In B J Fogg's research at the Behavior Design Lab at Stanford, they have found that even a tiny celebration after successfully doing a habit can trigger positive endorphins and encourage our brain to encode and repeat the behaviour (Fogg, 2020).

Katy Milkman at the University of Pennsylvania proposes the concept of temptation bundling – where you combine a habit that you don't want to do with something that you enjoy. Along with some colleagues, Milkman led a study to test out temptation bundling. They had gym goers sign up to participate and either get access to an iPod with audio books of the participant's choosing pre-loaded, only available when they were at the gym vs the control group where participants received a gift certificate and could purchase their own audiobooks, which they may or may not use at the gym, but this was not suggested. In this study, they tracked the participants' gym participation and found gym participation for those who had the pre-loaded iPods accessible only at the gym (forced temptation bundling) had 55 per cent higher gym participation rate than the control group. In a follow-up study, even just teaching people about temptation bundling and suggesting the use of audio books at the gym led to a 7 per cent higher participation rate than those who were not told about temptation bundling (Milkman, 2021).

Whether it's a small celebration such as saying to ourselves 'good job', or a big smile or doing a fist pump, such as B J Fogg recommends, or whether it's temptation bundling (allowing ourselves access to something we enjoy, only when we're doing something we need to do), we do better when we enjoy things. In learning, we can use simple things like encouraging people to temptation bundle – when they are out on a walk they can listen to a podcast – or having fun learning contests periodically to award simple points or prizes for learning. Even just making people aware of the need for fun and encouraging them to build it into their learning routine can help. With that in mind, remember: **To get it done, make it fun.**

TABLE 4.1 A – Allow for feeling good

AUTOMATIC	Remember ...
Allow for feeling good – We do better when we enjoy things.	To get it done, make it fun.

*U*nder the influence

The second letter is U. The U in AUTOMATIC stands for 'Under the influence'. We are influenced more by people we like, and by experts, or leaders, especially if we like them. We know that charismatic leaders who are well liked do better even if they are less competent than less appealing leaders. We are influenced by expertise as we select products to buy – if an actor is wearing a white coat in an ad for a health product, we are more likely to rate the product favourably and more likely to purchase, even when we know the person is an actor and not a medical expert (Cialdini, 2021).

You've probably noticed influence in your work – are you more likely to follow through on a suggestion if you receive a note about it from the executive leader of your division or if you receive a note from a colleague? What about if it's a colleague that you like and admire vs one that you don't like?

In an effort to reduce the amount of time and thinking we need to do to judge the merit of a suggestion, we use evidence of expertise (such as titles, dress, confidence) of the person asking as a proxy to judge the validity of their request. In the words of the singer Meghan Trainor, 'Give me that title, title', we rely on titles to judge people's requests – often as a shortcut despite when our own expertise would tell us to do something different. For example, in a study, nurses in a hospital received a call from someone identifying themselves as a doctor, requesting that the nurse deliver an unusual and large amount of medication to a patient. A total of 95 per cent of the nurses complied with the request, despite the request coming through a phone call from someone they didn't know and for an amount of a drug that was more than usually prescribed. A person from the study intervened before they actually delivered the medication. The nurses complied with the request because the person on the phone said they were a doctor (Hofling et al, 1966). Pressed for time in a busy hospital environment, they used the title as a shortcut to decide to act on the request; they probably also judged the tone and manner of the speaker to decide if it was a valid request. We are influenced by titles, expertise and the likability of the person asking us to do something.

In another study, people were asked to give a dime to someone who was short on change for their parking meter. Half of the people were asked by someone in plain street clothes, and half were asked by someone in a security guard uniform. Those asked by the guard nearly all complied, even when the requestor was no longer watching; but less than half did so when asked by someone in plain clothes (Bushman, 1988). We use clothing as a proxy to judge the validity of the request, and we're often very unaware that we do this.

In organizational learning, we can use this mental shortcut to nudge people to learn, by being aware of who is sending the message about learning. Are they seen as an expert by the audience? Are they well-liked in the organization? Are they in a leadership position and likely to be successful as an influencer? Does the tone of the message make the requestor likeable? Remember that we're under the influence. In other words, **if the leader is a gem, we'll follow them.**

TABLE 4.2 U – Under the Influence

AUTOMATIC	Remember ...
Under the influence – We are influenced more by people we like, and by experts, or leaders.	If the leader is a gem, we'll follow them.

*T*ip the scale

The next letter in our AUTOMATIC mnemonic is T, for 'Tip the scale'. We use social proof – what other people are doing – as a short-cut to decide to do something. It will tip the scale to get us to move forward. When we want to decide something quickly, we often look to what other people, particularly other people like us, are doing and then we follow that as a proxy for validity. We are social creatures and the ability to co-operate as a group and collaborate is a strength that has helped build up society and make humans the dominant species on the planet (Bregman, 2020).

We may not even realize we are using social proof as a quick-thinking shortcut. After all, many of us remember being asked if we would jump off a cliff if everyone else did, when adults were trying to persuade us to avoid peer pressure as a teenager. And while we may get smarter about deciding things on our own, for many quick deci-sions that are low value, we use social proof to help us. That's why on Amazon, you'll see 'Others who bought this, also looked at this', and on Netflix, we see suggestions for viewing based on what others like us viewed.

One campaign shows this very effectively. To encourage seatbelt use, a social campaign was launched to let people know that most people use seatbelts. A survey indicated that 85 per cent of people used their seatbelt but thought that only 60 per cent of people generally did. The campaign let people know the true proportion of people using seatbelts and as a result seatbelt use increased significantly (Dolan et al, 2010).

In another example of the power of making social norms visible, a restaurant labelled their most popular dish as most popular on their menu. Seeing that this dish was popular convinced even more people to buy it, and they saw the sale of that particular menu item increase (Cialdini, 2021). It's also very effective when we see an indicator of popularity that doesn't appear to be designed to promote demand – for example, Toyota saw an increase in sales when they advertised that they were so busy they needed more sales people (Cialdini, 2021).

With learning in organizations, especially when it is continuous learning done individually, it is hard to see social proof of learning. We don't see evidence of other people learning, like we would if we were all in a classroom session together. With continuous learning, making the learning visible and providing social proof of learning is very powerful. Sharing quotes about how people applied the learning, sharing successes of learning at town hall meetings and having people just talk about what they are learning in a quick lightening round in a team meeting, can all help provide social proof of learning and establish the social norm for learning in the organization. Remember: **If we can't see it, we often won't do it.**

TABLE 4.3 T – Tip the Scale

AUTOMATIC	Remember ...
Tip the scale – We are influenced by what others are doing so make social proof of learning habits visible.	If we don't see it, we often won't do it.

*O*wnership

O is for Ownership. Our sense of ownership greatly increases the value we put on something. We attribute greater value to something simply because we own it, in part because we would feel the pain of giving it up (Kahneman, 2013). You may have noticed this yourself – for example, many people will think their own house is worth a certain amount, but then are disappointed when they have an appraisal by a realtor who says it is worth less than they expected, based on comparable houses in the market. They had attributed more value to the house, with any flaws it may have, simply because they own it.

We feel an increased sense of ownership if we had a hand in creating the item – for example, in studies people have attributed more value to items if they had to assemble the item themselves. This has led to the effect being dubbed the IKEA effect.

In learning, the sense of ownership may include our current skill set, which may lead people to overvalue their current skills and undervalue any new skills they may actually need to acquire. But we can also look at the IKEA effect – if people invest time and energy in building their skills, they will see them as more valuable. It is worthwhile to remember this sense of ownership as we build programmes or message the audience about continuous learning. Remember: **If it's mine, I think it's super fine.**

TABLE 4.4 O – Ownership

AUTOMATIC	Remember ...
Ownership – We attribute greater value to something simply because we own it.	If it's mine, I think it's super fine.

*M*indset

The M is for Mindset. A large influence on our motivations is our mindset. Carol Dweck coined the term 'growth mindset' and has studied and written extensively on growth mindset vs fixed mindset

(Dweck, 2006). You may already be familiar with the concept as growth mindset is a very popular concept that has inspired company-wide training programmes.

For those newer to the idea, growth mindset is the framework of embracing the process of improving and learning skills; feedback is encouraged that fosters reflection and recognition of the process and strategies involved in improving or working on challenges. Someone with a growth mindset embraces new experiences for learning and sees failures, not as an indication that they lack skills but as an indication that they can develop the skills.

A fixed mindset, on the other hand, is when people think in terms of fixed traits, as in 'I am smart' or 'I am fast' and while this may sound confident and positive, it can lead people to avoid activities where they may not appear smart or be fast. They avoid challenges or opportunities for improvement if they perceive it may call into question their fixed sense of competence. Feedback that praises characteristics like, 'You did that math problem, you're so smart' fosters a fixed mindset.

Why does this matter for continuous learning in organizations? It matters because if your programme or messaging triggers a fixed mindset in people, they will avoid any activities that may call their competence into question. Instead, we want to ensure that people think in terms of a growth mindset, and that they embrace their development as the thing that they own (ownership effect), and they look to build their skills through continuous learning. The workplace is especially prone to a fixed mindset as people have built up their professional reputation, and they are very sensitive to anything that may harm that reputation or call it into question.

When we put the added pressure of the uncertainty of the future of work on them, perhaps inadvertently through programme messaging, then they may react defensively and feel even more fixed in their mindset. Instead, we need to be aware of the messages we're sending and ensure they foster a growth mindset and sense of excitement about personal development. Remember: **As my skill set grows, my fixed mindset will decompose.**

TABLE 4.5 M – Mindset

AUTOMATIC	Remember ...
Mindset – We need to own our development, not our fixed skill set.	As my skill set grows, my fixed mindset will decompose.

Avoid losses

The other A in the mnemonic stands for 'Avoid losses'. In our mental shortcuts, we attribute more value to the fear of a loss than the positivity of a potential gain. In studies, this shows as we will worry more about the potential to lose $100 than the potential to gain $100. Daniel Kahneman and Amos Tversky named this loss avoidance Prospect Theory and wrote a seminal work on it that helped kick start the field of behavioural economics (Kahneman, 2013).

When you combine a fixed mindset with ownership and our loss avoidance, you can see you have a powerful reason for people to avoid learning opportunities at work. People want to protect their reputation, they don't want to do anything that may cause their current skill set to be questioned, so they have a fixed mindset on their skills and seek to avoid any losses. Add to that, the reporting and analytics available to organizations when learning moves to continuous hybrid learning with online options, and you have even more employees avoiding something that will show a report that questions their sense of self (fixed mindset), may cause them a loss in reputation (loss aversion) and undervalues their current skill set (ownership). While organizations may want to focus on the analytics and reporting available, employees may be questioning if this is a way they want to learn.

With our need to avoid losses, we need to ensure that employees do not risk their reputation or skill set by engaging in continuous learning. Learning should be something that is seen as a positive activity, with the opportunity to gain new skills. Messaging should reinforce that learning is an opportunity to try new things, experiment and that a safe learning environment is available. After all, remember: **Don't ignore a potential gain just because a loss would be a pain.**

TABLE 4.6 A – Avoid losses

AUTOMATIC	Remember ...
Avoid losses – We seek to avoid losses more than we look to receive gains.	Don't ignore a potential gain just because a loss would be a pain.

*T*owards the default

The next letter in AUTOMATIC is T for 'Towards the default'. There are many demands on our attention at work. Even more so during COVID and the shift to remote or hybrid work, we have extensive demands on our time from both paid work and our lives at home. Mental shortcuts are absolutely needed to help us manage the many demands on our time. One of the most powerful mental shortcuts is that we tend to go with the default. When faced with a choice, we often stick with whatever is pre-chosen for us – whatever is the default.

Richard Thaler and Cass Sunstein outline a great example of this in their book *Nudge*. In a study done on retirement savings participation, employees who were automatically opted in to the retirement savings plan, with the option to select to opt out, tended to stay with the default and participate in the retirement savings programme. In organizations where people had to choose to opt in for the retirement savings programme, and fill in paperwork to participate, there was far less participation for retirement savings (Thaler and Sunstein, 2009).

If we can make the best option the default option, we'll get more people participating. And this doesn't have to be with systems – if we make it easy to do something, we'll go with it by default. In learning programmes, this can mean opting people into the learning systems instead of requiring them to request access. It can mean sending a calendar invite to block time for learning instead of expecting people to block time themselves. Wherever we can make the desired behaviour the default, the better the participation will be. Remember: **To be quick, go with the default pick.**

TABLE 4.7 T – Towards the default

AUTOMATIC	Remember ...
Towards the default – We go with the default option – so make it easy to go with the choice that does us the most good.	To be quick, go with the default pick.

Incentives

Next is I for Incentives. Another influence on our decisions is incentives. We like to get a reward for doing things and we tend to like short-term rewards more than long-term rewards in general. This is evidenced in studies where people are offered a short-term incentive to do something or a larger incentive further down the road – most people go with the short-term offering (Dolan et al, 2010).

Does this sound familiar? Would you rather have a Starbucks today or put the coffee money into a retirement savings plan? Most people go for the Starbucks today rather than saving for retirement. Studies even show that we have trouble considering our future selves as an actual person. We undervalue something that will benefit our future selves and overvalue something that will benefit our present selves (Hershfield, 2013).

In learning, this can mean that our messaging about career growth and future opportunities does not resonate with the audience. We can work to help them fully picture themselves in the future to help them recognize the value of the long term-incentives. We can also use short-term incentives – for example, a campaign with the chance to win prizes, then we'll likely get more interest from the same people. Short-term incentives can even induce us to disregard our loss aversion – as we may put our fixed mindset and sense of ownership aside for a quick reward now. While we can't always offer rewards for learning, nor would we want to, we can be careful not to have messaging that overvalues the future selves of our audiences, when they are really focused on the value to their present self. There's a reason we have the saying – remember – **A bird in the hand is worth two in the bush.**

TABLE 4.8 | – Incentives

AUTOMATIC	Remember ...
Incentives – We are influenced by incentives, and we overvalue short-term incentives over long-term incentives even to the extent that we will give up a higher-value incentive in favour of a lower-value short-term incentive.	A bird in the hand is worth two in the bush.

Commitment

The last letter in our AUTOMATIC mnemonic is C for 'Continue the commitment'. As we are social creatures, and we have a strong sense of self, we like to be consistent with commitments we've made to ourselves, and we care even more if we made commitments in front of other people. We don't like to be inconsistent – we'll change what we're thinking just to line up consistently.

If we make a commitment, we like to be consistent with that previous commitment. We use this as a shortcut in a lot of our thinking. For example, we may have an opinion on a particular policy, but rather than sticking with that opinion, in studies, where a policy is presented that doesn't align with our own views, but it is indicated that people from our political party agree with the policy, we are more likely to change our stance and agree with the policy. We use our previous decision (which political party we like) as a short cut for future decisions. This allows us to make quick choices and to stay consistent in our party choice (Cialdini, 2021). We also like to be consistent with our view of ourselves, for example if we think of ourselves as a voter (vs asking if we are going to vote), we are more likely to vote if we view ourselves as a voter (Cialdini, 2016).

This also applies to small starts – for example, people who were asked to put a small sign in their window, were more likely to later put up a lawn sign supporting the same cause, because they had already agreed before to the smaller request (Cialdini, 2021). We see con artists take advantage of this – for example, the Netflix show *The Tinder Swindler* shares the story of a man who asked his various girlfriends for larger and larger amounts of money – in part because they didn't want to be inconsistent, many of them agreed.

In learning, we can use this 'continue the commitment' device in a positive way to nudge people to learn. Encouraging teams to talk about learning and have people pair up to hold each other accountable can be a powerful strategy to help people commit and follow through on learning. Remember: **If I say it, I better do it.**

TABLE 4.9 C – Commitment

AUTOMATIC	Remember ...
Commitment – We like to be consistent with our commitments – and we do this even more if we have shared our commitment with someone else.	If I say it, I better do it.

Making habits AUTOMATIC

As we look at learning habits in the subsequent chapters, I'll share tips aligned with each letter of AUTOMATIC. It will form a checklist to use to help you make learning habits more successful for your yourself or your audience.

There is a wealth of research on how we behave, the shortcuts we use in our thinking – I've included highlights here. We shouldn't leave it to just persuasive technology firms like Facebook and TikTok to use these insights to hook us. We can use them for driving learning habits. Learning is a worthwhile endeavour that warrants the use of ethically designed nudges to help people learn. If you don't have PhDs on staff with behavioural insights expertise, a quick way to get started and use the insights is to apply AUTOMATIC as a checklist to change behaviour for good.

Key takeaways

Here is the full list of AUTOMATIC and the rhyming phrases to help you remember each item.

TABLE 4.10 Make habits AUTOMATIC

AUTOMATIC	Remember ...
Allow for feeling good – We do better when we enjoy things	*To get it done, make it fun.*
Under the influence – We are influenced more by people we like, and by experts, or leaders.	*If the leader is a gem, we'll follow them.*
Tip the scale – We are influenced by what others are doing so make social proof of learning habits visible.	*If we don't see it, we'll skip it.*
Ownership – We attribute greater value to something simply because we own it.	*If it's mine, I think it's super fine.*
Mindset – We need to own our development, not our fixed skill set.	*As my skill set grows, my fixed mindset will decompose.*
Avoid losses – We seek to avoid losses more than we look to receive gains.	*Don't ignore a potential gain just because a loss would be a pain.*
Towards the default – We go with the default option – so make it easy to go with the choice that does us the most good.	*To be quick, go with the default pick.*
Incentives – We are influenced by incentives, and we overvalue short-term incentives over long-term incentives even to the extent that we will give up a higher-value incentive in favour of a lower-value short-term incentive.	*A bird in the hand is worth two in the bush.*
Commitment – We like to be consistent with our commitments – and we do this even more if we have shared our commitment with someone else.	*If I say it, I better do it.*

Questions to ask yourself

- For the cognitive shortcuts outlined in AUTOMATIC, how many of these resonate with you?

- With AUTOMATIC, how many of these are you currently using in fostering learning in your organization or in your team?

- As you go through the next week, observe your behaviour and the behaviour of others. How often do you see elements of AUTOMATIC at work?

- When you consider your home life, how could you use AUTOMATIC to help yourself gain habits that support your goals?

References

Bregman, R (2020) *Humankind: A hopeful history*, Little Brown and Company, New York

Bushman, B J (1988) The effects of apparel on compliance: A field experiment with a female authority figure. *Personality and Social Psychology Bulletin*, **14** (3), 459–467

Cialdini, R (2016) *Pre-suasion: A revolutionary way to influence and persuade*, Simon and Schuster Paperbacks, New York

Cialdini, R B (2021) *Influence: The psychology of persuasion – new and expanded*, Harper Business, New York

Dolan, P, Hallsworth, M, Halpern, D, King, D and Metcalfe, R (2010) *Mindspace: Influencing behavior through public policy*, Institute for Government, London

Duckworth, A L, Milkman, K L and Laibson, D (2018) Beyond willpower: strategies for reducing failures of self control. *Psychological Science in the Public Interest*, **19** (3), pp 102–129.

Dweck, C (2006) *Mindset: The new psychology of success*, Ballentine Books, s.l.

Fogg, B (2020) *Tiny Habits: The small changes that change everything*, Houghton Mifflin Harcourt, New York

Henrich, J (2020) *The Weirdest People in the World: How the West became psychologically peculiar and particularly prosperous*, Farrar Straus and Giroux, New York

Hershfield, H (2013) You make better decisions if you 'see' your senior self, *Harvard Business Review*, June.

Hofling, C K, Brotzman, E, Dalrymple, S, Graves, N and Bierce, C (1966) An experimental study of nurse-physician relations. *Journal of Nervous and Mental Disease*, **143**, 171–180

Kahneman, D (2013) *Thinking Fast and Slow*, Anchor Canada.

Milkman, K (2021) *How to Change: The science of getting from where you are to where you want to be*, Portfolio Penguin, New York

Thaler, R H and Sunstein, C R (2009) *Nudge: Improving decisions about health, wealth and happiness.* Penguin, New York

05

The LEARN model

We have seen the importance of habits and been introduced to how to make habits automatic, but how do we put this all together, and what does it look like at an organization level? Let's dive into how to put it all together now.

Putting it all together

The learning habits in this book can each be used as a stand-alone, but if you want to move to a learning culture, you'd want to combine various habits to encourage more learning across the organization. You need to first determine your current state and have a vision for your future state for habits across the organization. In order to have a common understanding to define your current stage and to collaborate with others on a vision for the future, a common framework and language is needed. We know from studies that if people are not working from the same reference point, it is hard to come to a common understanding and agreement on moving forward (Livingstone, 2021). We need to have a common frame of reference in order to discuss where we are, and where we want to get to.

In addition, when we seek to come to a common understanding, especially in the context of decision-making, we want to assess the probability of items to occur. In speaking about probability and determining our current state, if we can use percentages instead of words to describe a situation, it provides a more comparable reference point (Duke, 2020).

As organizations vary so much and have different goals and needs, a definition of a learning culture on a graduated scale is much more customizable to the organization's needs and gives us a way to judge the current state and determine where we want to get to, all the time working from a shared understanding instead of mixed mental models of people's vague ideas of a learning culture.

By looking at what people are actually doing in organizations that supports learning – their learning habits – and then looking at how many people are using the habits, how often they are using the habits and the variety of habits used, we can create a model that is flexible to what organizations are striving towards. The LEARN model for learning habits helps you do just that.

The LEARN model provides a way to rate your organization, teams and individuals on learning habits – from a frequency, ubiquity and depth view. As we saw in Chapter 2, the definition of a learning culture is based on the use of learning habits. Once you determine where you are currently, you can look to move forward to your next desired state.

FIGURE 5.1 What makes a learning culture?

Frequency (how often are learning habits occurring?)

Ubiquity (how much of the organization is using the learning habits?)

Depth (how many learning habits are occurring?)

= Learning Culture

Each of the five stages in the LEARN model is based on the percentages of adoption across the areas defining a learning culture. Let's examine this.

LEARN model: five stages

The LEARN model is a five-stage model that defines what a learning culture, based on learning habits, looks like at each stage. Let's look at each level separately and then look at the measurements for each level.

1. Lifting stage

The first stage is the Lifting stage. At this stage in the model, habits are used zero to 20 per cent of the time across 0 to 20 per cent of the organization, and only 0 to 20 per cent of the habits you are targeting are in use at all. So what does that mean? If your organization has not yet identified target learning habits, and if your teams are using learning habits organically, without any strategy or corporate drive behind them, and if these organic habits are in use across just a few teams, and only some of the time, that would put you in the Lifting stage. Many small companies without formal learning and development (L&D) departments to support learning, and where management coaching is not formalized, would fall into this category. When you're in the Lifting stage, the roles across your organization are not yet working formally to support learning habits. They would look like this:

Executive guidance

At this stage, the organization may have a formal learning and development department, but they are not focused on learning habits at all; the organization may be more focused on event-based learning and executives are not yet aware of the need to drive learning habits.

Programme management

In the Lifting stage, learning is most likely focused on onboarding and compliance learning. There are no programmes yet in place with a focus on continuous learning, so the programme manager role is more likely to be focused on sales enablement, onboarding or compliance learning and is done by an HR business partner or potentially by a sales enablement professional.

Administration

In the Lifting stage, the organization is unlikely to have systems for learning specifically, but if there are, the administration is focused on compliance and onboarding learning, not on continuous learning or learning habits.

Communications

There may be a corporate communications function but the HR/ Learning group is not yet partnering with them for learning initiatives. There is no formal plan for communicating learning opportunities or continuous learning in the organization.

Line of business executive

Line of business executives are not yet focused on supporting learning within their organization, though a few executives may be driving this for their groups based on their past experience and personal belief in the value of learning at work.

Manager

Managers have access to some leadership learning from the company, but there are no formal resources or strategic plan for continuous learning. Some managers may be driving learning habits in their group as a result of their personal beliefs and management style, but it is not an expectation or a supported activity in the company.

Individual contributor

Individuals may have their own personal learning habits, but the organization does not support time or model behaviours for learning habits, so individuals most likely confine their learning to their own time and focused on their own interests. On a case-by-case basis, they may get access to learning for their role if their manager is supportive. This learning is most likely event driven and done off-site, with the exception of compliance and onboarding learning at work.

Overall, at the Lifting stage, we expect to see learning habits 0 to 20 per cent of the time, across less than 20 per cent of the organization and with only a few learning habits in use (less than 20 per cent of the habits outlined in this book).

2. Emerging stage

In the Emerging stage, there is recognition by the organization that continuous learning is needed. Systems may have been put in place to support continuous learning, such as learning experience platforms or learning management systems. There may not yet be a strategy for continuous learning in the organization, but habits are growing as a result of pointed effort, not just organically.

As we look at roles in this stage of learning, they are different than in the Lifting stage and show a more concerted effort to support a learning culture. The company may even include some learning metrics in their annual report, as well as their annual planning. The roles at this stage look like the following:

Executive guidance

In the Emerging stage, there is most likely an executive responsible for learning – this could be a Chief Learning Officer, a VP of Learning and Development or a Chief Talent Officer. This executive is setting the strategy for continuous learning for the organization, in line with the priorities set out annually by the CEO. Executives set the expectation and model of the behaviour, some of the time, for learning habits.

Programme management

At this stage, there are a number of learning programmes that have shifted from event-based to continuous learning offerings. The programme managers responsible for these programmes sometimes think about how to design for learning habits, but they are mostly focused on the success of the specific programmes they are responsible for.

Administration

At this point, as there are most likely systems in place for access to learning, there is someone responsible for the administration of these systems (there may be multiple people or even a department within HR for analytics). At this stage, they are asked for ad-hoc reporting on analytics in support of learning habits but the organization is not yet formalized or decided on how they would measure learning habits. They may use surveys to ask employees about their habits, perhaps as a subsection of their employee engagement survey.

Communications

During this stage, there is a formal corporate communications department, and they are sometimes tasked with supporting learning messaging. It is most likely on an event-driven basis or as part of a specific learning programme. They are not yet supporting an ongoing learning culture communication strategy.

Line of business expertise

While in the Emerging stage, the learning executive seeks out champions from within the lines of business, and encourages them to message and support continuous learning in their groups. Therefore, at this stage, we start to see learning councils or communities of practice formed, with representatives from various lines of business involved in supporting continuous learning in their business groups.

Managers

At this point, managers are supported with coaching materials and leadership learning to help them support their groups in ongoing learning. There is an expectation that they coach and message their group to encourage ongoing learning, most likely in line with the performance management cycle.

Individual contributors

During this phase, individual contributors may have their own learning habits, but they are increasingly supported in identifying how to continue learning in line with their team's and their specific role's priorities. They may have a manager who is supportive of learning and they may hear from executives about the organization's support for a learning culture.

Overall, in the Emerging stage, we see learning habits across 20 to 40 per cent of the organization, the variety of learning habits has increased with 20 to 40 per cent of the targeted learning habits in use. The groups that are using learning habits use them about 20 to 40 per cent of the time. This is measured by systems in place, key performance indicators, and can be assessed by a survey of the organization.

3. Aligning stage

The Aligning stage is characterized by a strategic and comprehensive approach to driving learning habits throughout the organization. Learning habits are frequent, ubiquitous and identified. Most likely there is a strong executive influence starting from the CEO to set the expectation for learning habits and model the behaviour. Learning is seen as a key competency of the organization, rather than something that the Learning and Development group is responsible for. Across the roles we've discussed here are how they work at this stage:

Executive guidance

In the Aligning stage, the executive team is in support of learning habits and continuous learning. There is most likely a VP of Learning or a Chief Learning Officer, but the executive team as a whole supports learning. It is likely that the CEO models continuous learning behaviour and has helped to build the culture of learning habits.

Programme management

During the Aligning stage, there are programme managers responsible for learning programmes, and there may be a programme manager responsible for driving continuous learning specifically. There is a strategy for continuous learning and responsibility for this strategy is resourced across programme managers or with one programme manager in particular.

Administration

While in this stage, there are learning systems in place and reporting is organized for showing learning value but reporting is not a focus of the learning habits. With the executive support and regular behaviours of learning habits, there is less of a need to prove that the habits are occurring through system reporting, rather the focus has shifted to reporting that shows the value of learning habits through links to key performance indicators from the business.

Communications

At this point, there is consistent and integrated messaging about learning habits. The communications function builds materials to support continuous learning and shares these so that managers and executives have what they need to be supporting effective habits in their groups as a part of how they do business.

Line of business expertise

In this stage, with the executive team setting the expectations and modelling the behaviour of learning habits, the lines of business also do the same for the most part. There may be a few lines of business who have a different approach in their groups, but on the whole the line of business expertise support, demonstrate and drive continuous learning in their groups.

Managers

While in this stage, nearly the majority of the managers support continuous learning on their teams. While some may have a different approach in their groups, for the most part, the expectations set and demonstrated by the executive team are supported and managed by the managers across the enterprise.

Individual contributors

During this phase, employees know what the expectation of the executive teams is in regards to continuous learning. For some employees, the message may not be as reinforced by their direct managers, so they are less likely to demonstrate learning behaviours, but for nearly the majority of teams, continuous learning is an expectation.

Overall in the Aligning stage the executive team is demonstrating their ongoing commitment to continuous learning, they ensure that learning helps to enable the organization to achieve their key performance indicators in line with the corporate strategy. Learning habits are in evidence across 40 to 60 per cent of the organization and done on a regular basis, and the habits are in line with the corporate strategy. Many organizations aspire to this level of continuous learning, but they lack the executive support and the organizational commitment to the time needed for supporting continuous learning.

4. Robust stage

In the Robust stage, learning habits are used in the majority of the organization, the organization has a variety of learning habits in use and the habits are in evidence the majority of the time. At this stage, there is ample social proof of the use of habits and it is part of the social norms of the organization to use learning habits. The support of learning habits goes across all levels of the organization and all roles. Let's dive into the key roles for supporting learning habits and how they show up at this stage:

Executive guidance

Executives demonstrate learning habits with their direct reports and they cascade the expectation of learning habits across the company. There is most likely a Chief Learning Officer, but they are by no means the only executive driving learning habits. The Chief Learning Officer leads the strategy for learning habits and has resources on their team to support them.

Programme management

In the robust stage, there is resourcing to include fostering continuous learning in the organization through learning habits. Programme managers shift from programme or project-based management of learning to a product owner mindset supporting the use of the continuous learning options.

Administration

The administration of continuous learning is linked to outcome metrics from the business. The administration ensures the access is smooth and fluid, reducing the energy to get to learning, and reporting is tied to business key performance indicators.

Communications

The communications role is used to regularly communicate about learning habits, share tools and support ongoing communication. The communications role is charged with supporting the strategy behind learning habits.

Line of business expertise

With the executive guidance firmly in place to support learning habits, the line of business expertise also demonstrates learning habits regularly. The use of learning habits is recognized as a worthwhile activity to drive key performance indicators. Learning habits may not even be outlined as anything other than 'the way we do business here', as the habits are an expectation based on the social norms established in the organization. In those groups where learning habits are less in evidence, they are expected to shift to adopt them.

Managers

With learning habits in evidence across the majority of the organization, and in evidence the majority of the time, managers are expected to support them in their groups. The onboarding and leadership training for managers will include resources and materials, as well as coaching, to support managers in driving learning habits in their organization. It is an expectation that learning habits are done so that the company and teams can achieve their key performance indicators.

Individual contributors

Individuals who join the organization soon see learning habits in evidence, as they are done the majority of the time. Individual contributors soon see that they are expected to integrate learning habits into their own individual way of working, and they see that they need to do that to level up their game, and achieve what is expected of them.

Overall, in the Robust stage, the executives support and demonstrate learning habits, it is a strategic support to how the company achieves their business outcomes, and the managers and individual contributors feel supported in learning habits. The habits are in evidence across 60 to 80 per cent of the organization, they are done 60 to 80 per cent of the time and the habits in evidence are numerous and strategically chosen to support the business.

5. Normalized stage

In the Normalized stage, learning habits are now the way of working for the entire organization. They are in evidence across all teams, and done over 80 per cent of the time, and the habits are extensive. The company culture embraces learning habits and uses them to support business outcomes, innovation and preparing for the future of work. Here's how learning habits are in evidence across the roles:

Executive guidance

In this stage, the executive team has ensured that habits are in evidence across all lines of business, and that they are practised at all levels of the organization. Most likely the company mission and values include behaviours that support learning habits and the company works hard to ensure people are supporting the mission and always demonstrating the values.

Programme management

The programme management works to support the mission and values and ensures that learning habits are done as part of this context. There is a focus on continuous learning through ongoing management and communication and there are resources dedicated to driving learning habits specifically.

Administration

The administration function is aligned to business key performance indicators and makes dashboards available with data analytics insight readily available to support business decisions. The focus of reporting is less on consumption of learning and more on results of learning aligned to key performance indicators from the business.

Communications

In the Normalized stage, communications support learning habits and enables all levels of the organization to have the communications materials they need to regularly and consistently drive learning habits. The communication function for learning habits has most likely moved over to the learning group rather than within the corporate communications function.

Line of business expertise

At this stage, all lines of business regularly demonstrate learning habits; it is an expectation of the business. The executives support their teams in demonstrating learning habits, and if a manager or team within a line of business is not demonstrating learning habits, there are systems and expectations in place to see this and address it.

Managers

Managers are coached on how to demonstrate and support learning habits; it is part of the mission and values and these are lived values they are expected to follow daily. There are systems and supports in place to ensure learning habits are integrated into the way people work. The context of the organization expects learning habits.

Individual contributors

Individual contributors are expected to regularly demonstrate the behaviours aligned to the values which in themselves drive learning habits. New employees quickly see that the context of the organization expects and promotes learning habits so employees develop their own individual habits as it is the social norm in the organization.

The Normalized stage shows how an organization can set the context for learning habits and integrate them at all levels. They can drive learning habits through their vision and values, and ensure the social norms in the organization make it difficult to not demonstrate learning habits. Learning habits are displayed across 80 to 100 per cent of the organization and they are done more than 80 per cent of the time. With the habits built into the mission and values, the habitual depth is above 80 per cent.

Now that we have dived deep into each level, here is a summary chart showing all of the levels with the frequency, ubiquity and habitual depth laid out for each level.

TABLE 5.1 The LEARN Model

	Frequency	Ubiquity	Habitual depth
Lifting 0–20%	Habits are displayed about 0–20% of the time	Habits are embedded in 0–20% of the organization	0–20% of the habits identified here are used in the organization
Emerging 21–40%	Habits are displayed about 21–40% of the time	Habits are embedded in 21–40% of the organization	21–40% of the habits identified here are used in the organization
Aligning 41–60%	Habits are displayed about 41–60% of the time	Habits are embedded in 41–60% of the organization	41–60% of the habits identified here are used in the organization
Robust 61–80%	Habits are displayed about 61–80% of the time	Habits are embedded in 61–80% of the organization	61–80% of the habits identified here are used in the organization
Normalized 81–100%	Habits are displayed about 81–100% of the time	Habits are embedded in 81–100% of the organization	81–100% of the habits identified here are used in the organization.

Having read through these stages now in this chapter and seeing the summary chart, you can rate your own organization on the frequency, ubiquity and habitual depth – are you at 40 per cent, 50 per cent or just starting at 10 per cent? Add up your rating across the three areas and then average the percentage to get your overall stage. For example, if your organization is has a learning habits frequency of 10 per cent, a ubiquity average of 40 per cent and an habitual depth of 60 per cent, the average would be 36 per cent, putting your company at the Emerging stage overall.

Key takeaways

- The LEARN model has five levels and the rating across frequency, ubiquity and habitual depth can give you an idea of where your own organization falls.

- You can see how executive guidance, programme management, administration, communication, line of business expertise, managers and individual contributors act at each stage of the LEARN model.
- You can use the model to help you assess your organization's current stage and have a vision of which stage you want to move to and what it will look like.

Questions to ask yourself

- Which stage of the LEARN model does your organization resemble? Which stage does your team resemble? As you read through the habits chapters, think about the LEARN model and start to identify where your organization falls on the model.
- For the roles identified in this chapter, which ones do you have in your organization and how do their current activities match or not match the descriptions at each stage of the LEARN model?

References

Duke, A (2020) *How to Decide: Simple tools for making better choices*, Portfolio, New York

Livingstone, R (2021) *The Conversation: How seeking and speaking the truth about racism can radically transform individuals and organizations*, Currency, New York

PART TWO

Organization habits

06

AIM to LEARN

A few years ago, a large telecommunication firm was looking at supplementing their resources for continuous learning for the IT department. They had a site with learning materials available. It was used as pre-requisite learning for some instructor-led courses, but the organization also wanted to ensure that they had learning to support their strategic initiatives. For a large global IT audience, how did they go about getting this organized? Let's revisit that a little later.

When you're designing for continuous learning, the process works a little differently than when you design an event-based programme. When you want to do a needs analysis and align to business outcomes, with event-based learning you design for a group of people for one point in time, designing the programme and then running the programme and doing an evaluation. When you design continuous learning, the design process needs to be ongoing and aligned to business initiatives in line with the annual planning cycle of the organization.

For most companies, this is a major shift for the way learning and development is managed. It is a different way of working with the business. When you get it right, it is a keystone habit for learning, as it has a ripple effect across all learning habits in the organization. So how do you do this type of design for continuous learning? What does this keystone habit look like?

Overview of the habit

The process of aligning continuous learning to the annual planning cycle and organizational initiatives is a new habit for those who have been aligning event-based learning per programme. It is a worthwhile endeavour to master as it makes you a partner with the business and integrated into the measurements that the business is targeting. By following this habit, you'll be in a much better position to share business results and the impact of learning with leadership.

Cue

As with any habit, it starts with a cue. **The start of the planning cycle is the cue** to book meetings with your key stakeholders. The planning cycle varies depending on the fiscal year of the organization. For companies with a year end at 31 December, they generally plan in August/September. For companies with a year end at 31 October, they generally start their planning in late May, early June. You can align with stakeholders at any time of the year, but it's a good idea to get an idea of what's coming for the next fiscal year by booking time with your stakeholders as they do their planning. You may want to book time with them for after they have completed their planning so that they know what their initiatives will be, but this only works if you can wait until then for your own planning.

Routine

The next step is the routine – using Align, Improve, Measure (AIM). This routine is what makes this a keystone habit as it can help your continuous learning to work in alignment with the organization and enables continuous improvement.

Align, Improve, Measure is a three-step process that provides you a way to design your learning with your stakeholders' expectations considered.

Align is the process of discovering what your stakeholders are planning. The questions you ask can become the agenda for the meeting with your stakeholders. You'll want to ensure that your stakeholders know what you'll be asking about ahead of time, so include an outline of the questions in your meeting invite. Here are the types of questions you'll want to ask:

- What are your key initiatives?
- Who are the key stakeholders and how would continuous learning support them?
- Who are the main audiences and what are their needs?
- What communication practices work well?
- What obstacles may appear?
- What would success look like? What key performance indicators would continuous learning support for your group?

When you're in the meeting with your stakeholders, it matters how you position the questions. Some participants may feel threatened by the questions or embarrassed at not knowing the initiatives for their business unit. They may misinterpret your questions and not answer at the level that you would like them to. They may only talk about the learning their group is requesting rather than sharing business initiatives. Some of these issues can be avoided if you share the questions ahead of time and provide the context for the questions. You can also help your stakeholders by having examples of the type of responses you're looking for – so they understand what type of information you're looking to uncover. Without this type of context, you may find your stakeholders will only share the type of learning they are looking for in their group, rather than discussing business initiatives. By having these types of discussions, you are helping to support the business as a trusted advisor, rather than simply hearing what training they want and delivering on that training. You are in alignment with what the business is trying to achieve.

For example, here is a story to illustrate this, based on real world events. A few years ago, a large pharmaceutical firm was planning a new type of continuous learning so there was a planning meeting with executives and the learning and development group. The questions above were shared ahead of time and discussed with the executives. When the meeting started though, the executives struggled to explain their initiatives and what the company wanted to achieve that year. They started responding about the types of learning the group needed, not what the company initiatives were. In this case, even though the questions had been shared ahead of time, there hadn't been enough context provided. After some discussion and sharing of examples, the meeting eventually got on track and the executives were able to share what their initiatives aligned to the corporate strategy were. But the misunderstanding could have been avoided, along with initial awkward discussion, if there had been a prep meeting with more context provided.

In contrast, at a financial services firm, the discussion with the executives went very smoothly. Again the questions were shared ahead of time. But during this meeting instead of just showing a slide with the question on it, a build slide was used that showed alignment to what level the questions were referring to. Per Figure 6.1, you can see the alignment of the questions to the level of the organization, and with a build starting at the CEO/CIO level, which makes for a much easier discussion. When this is supplemented with examples from similar organizations, it makes it much easier to have a productive discussion.

FIGURE 6.1   Align: this forms the basis for the Align meeting with stakeholders, and forms a key part of the routine of this habit

4. Success Criteria / Key Performance Indicators

3. Managers & Employees

2. Senior Leadership

1. CEO / CXO

4. What success criteria or key performance indicators apply to continuous learning?

3. Who are the main audiences and what are their needs? What communication practices work well? What obstacles may appear?

2. Who are the key stakeholders and how would continuous learning support them?

1. What are your key initiatives?

Improve

With the information uncovered in your Align meeting, you can begin to mock up a plan for supporting continuous learning in the group. At this stage, you don't need a perfect plan but you can mock up how continuous learning will be aligned to the initiatives and how it will be communicated to the audience. This mock-up can form your skeletal plan that you can then share with the stakeholders to ensure you get their buy-in and feedback for adjustments. The plan can take a few forms but will generally include how you are aligning available learning assets to the initiatives that you've discussed. It will include how you'll communicate to the audience about what is available to them, and it will incorporate what you've learned about typical communication methods and anticipated obstacles. It can include how you'll demonstrate executive support and what time is dedicated for learning for the audience. You can share the plan in the form of a timeline for the year, to give highlights of events and have a one-slide view that you can share back with stakeholders. This is a minimum viable product (MVP) – a plan that gives you the basics of what you need without being fully developed – so you can get feedback and iterate on what you have.

With your MVP plan ready, you can then share back this plan with your stakeholders and get their feedback. You would also confirm the key performance indicators that are aligned to your plan, to ensure that you have captured that information accurately. Once you have feedback, you can adjust your plan and begin.

Measure

With your Improve plan aligned with your stakeholders, you can begin implementing and measuring. As you have confirmation of the key performance indicators from your stakeholders, you can ensure that you are able to get insight into the progress on the key performance indicators (KPIs). You may want to set up quarterly meetings with your stakeholders in order to check in on progress and align on the measurements. This will help you to ensure you are staying on track and that the plan is working as intended. The process of aligning, improving and measuring is ongoing. Beginning in the planning phase of the fiscal year, you'll want to implement your plans and ensure that you have ongoing insight to measurements to check the progress of your plans. The plans and related measurements can be used as an input for the next cycle of planning for the new year.

AIM is a keystone habit

By using Align, Improve, Measure, you can ensure that your work is on track with what the organization is planning and the measurements that matter to the business. The process helps you to be a trusted advisor, proactively seeking out feedback on what the initiatives are for the year, rather than waiting for groups to come to you with learning requests. You can use AIM to find out what is planned for the year and ensure that continuous learning is available and aligned to what the organization needs. You can get feedback on your plans for the year. The learning habits that you are looking to foster in the organization will be supported by this process. This planning will have a ripple effect across all the learning habits in the organization – as it can inform your communications, your learning alignment and more. In this way it is a keystone habit.

Reward

By following this routine, you will understand your stakeholders' expectations and set aside time to mutually align on a plan. You'll be set up for success for fostering continuous learning in the organization. You'll be able to help support the group in achieving their key performance indicators. And by doing this, you'll be able to achieve your own key performance indicators as a learning and development lead for your organization.

FIGURE 6.2   Align, Improve and Measure: use AIM as part of your annual planning cycle with either data or expectation measures for continuous improvement

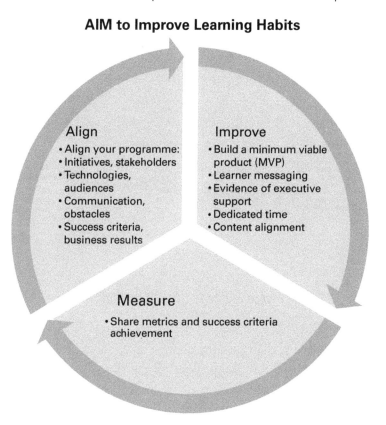

AIM to Improve Learning Habits

Align
- Align your programme:
- Initiatives, stakeholders
- Technologies, audiences
- Communication, obstacles
- Success criteria, business results

Improve
- Build a minimum viable product (MVP)
- Learner messaging
- Evidence of executive support
- Dedicated time
- Content alignment

Measure
- Share metrics and success criteria achievement

Context

AIM to LEARN helps to support a context in the organization where continuous learning is integrated into the planning cycle of the organization, rather than being done as an afterthought. Both formal and informal learning is planned in line with the priorities for the year. AIM and the iterative process it encourages helps to ensure that learning stays on track throughout the year. We know that changes happen and things do not always go to plan, but with this process you can stay more aligned to what your stakeholders need to achieve and ensure that learning is helping to support key initiatives.

FIGURE 6.3 AIM to LEARN habit

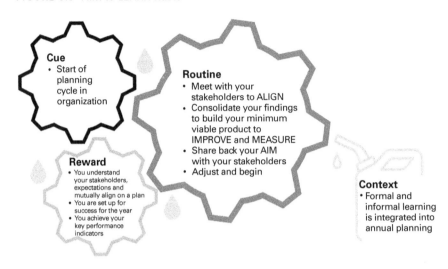

Measurement for the habit

With AIM to LEARN, in following the process the measurement for your overall plan is built into the process. You check with your stakeholders about their view of success during the Align meetings, and you ask about the key performance indicators that they need to achieve. This helps to ensure that your plans are on track. As recommended earlier, you can schedule quick check-ins with your stakeholders to align with them quarterly on the progress, if not more often. You'll want to get access to tracking for the key performance indicators so that you can see progress on those metrics.

For measuring the habit itself, you can set a goal for the depth and breadth of stakeholders you'll engage with. For example, you could have a goal of meeting with one stakeholder for each division you are working with. You could also set a goal for the number of follow-up meetings that you target to have – not all stakeholders will be available for follow-up meetings, either to review the plan or to engage quarterly in check-ins. Set a realistic expectation for your first time doing this and go from there.

Other ways you can measure your use of this habit include:

- number of stakeholders engaged
- number of meetings for Align discussions
- number of reviewed plans
- number of check-ins on progress
- achievement on key performance indicators
- execution of the plans – number of aligned programmes, success of communication tactics, surveys of audience

Ensure that you are measuring things that make a difference and that you're not having meetings for the sake of meetings. The number of stakeholders and the number of meetings matter less than the achievement against aligned KPIs. In addition, your audience will care more about the formal and informal learning offerings if they know how they align to the key performance indicators they are responsible for.

Make this habit AUTOMATIC

As with each habit in this book, let's look at how to make this one automatic. We can use the research on how we behave to suggest ways to make this habit stick.

A – Allow for feeling good. With this habit, make the planning sessions as engaging as possible. Try to get to know your stakeholders so that you can enjoy meeting and working with them. It can help to include some non-work topics at the beginning of the meeting to connect on a different level – perhaps some shared interests or even something as simple as chatting about upcoming time off, recent events or other areas of mutual interest.

When you've done your stakeholder meetings, congratulate yourself. Think about how you got the meetings done and do a simple reward like checking them off your list, thinking through what went well. And when you've completed your draft plans, give yourself a little break – do something you enjoy like going for a walk or getting a coffee with a colleague.

U – Under the influence. Some stakeholders will be more interested in this process than others. Remember that we're open to influence and your stakeholders are no exception. You can casually mention another stakeholder that you recently met with and share how that session went well. The reluctant participant may not show it, but they are probably influenced by what their peers are doing, so let them know that others are participating as well.

T – Tip the scale. The planning process and AIM overall isn't always seen within the organization. It can help people to participate if they see that it is the social norm to do so. Share examples of previous planning or discussions in line with this process as you speak with stakeholders. This can be as simple as referencing previous meetings in your email reach out to book sessions or when you're speaking with a new stakeholder to explain what type of meeting you're asking for. Remember that if we can't see it, we often won't do it, so make it seen as much as possible.

O – Ownership. One way to encourage stakeholders to participate in this process is to recognize success. As we know from Daniel Kahneman, we attribute more value to items simply because we own them (Kahneman, 2013). Recognize this with your stakeholders by mentioning their success and complimenting them on results from their group.

M – Mindset. The process of aligning with stakeholders can be uncomfortable, especially when the process is new or people are unsure what you are asking about. If a stakeholder is new to the process, have a quick prep meeting with them before the Align session so you can walk them through what you're going to be covering in the meeting. Sometimes you may find that people don't have the information you're looking for yet, so they can let you know their timing for getting it. They may be too early in the planning process to know what initiatives are planned. By having a quick prep meeting, you will help them get comfortable with the content of the meeting and they'll be better prepared for the session when you discuss plans, which will help you both get more out of it.

A – Avoid losses. We know that people will worry about losses more than they will value gains. Be cognizant of this when you are scheduling your Align meetings. You need to be aware of who will be grouped in the meeting and whether they will be comfortable together in this type of discussion. In addition to helping people understand the context, you'll want to ensure that if there is a group together in the meeting, that everyone is comfortable discussing these types of things together. If some people feel they will look bad in front of their colleague during the meeting, perhaps by not having the insight on initiatives, then they may avoid the meeting rather than sharing what they do know and risking a loss of reputation in front a colleague. Be sensitive to any groupings where participants may fear a loss of reputation.

T – Towards the default. Make it easy for your stakeholders to work with you. If you can have a draft plan already built that you can customize, that will set the expectation for what could be done and make it easier for the stakeholder to work with you. They can default to the sample plan that you have. This can also work for the initiatives and key performance indicators – if you have examples already this will either jog their memory or allow them to agree.

I – Incentives. Be kind to yourself as you go through this process. Think of ways you can give yourself incentives to get it done. They don't have to be big – a fist pump, a big smile, checking off the item on your to do list – just short recognition that you completed a component can give you a shot of dopamine and you'll feel the reward.

C – Commitment. When you meet with your stakeholders, commit to timing for having a draft plan to share with them. By committing to your timeframe in front of your stakeholders, you are much more likely to achieve it. In addition, if you can have their commitment to work together on the plan during the year, you'll be able to both hold each other accountable and you'll have a much higher chance of success (Kander, 2022).

YOUR ACTION PLAN

Now that you've read through this habit and the tools and technique involved, ask yourself these questions:

- Are you already doing this in your organization?

- Is there an effective cue for this habit? Do you know the planning cycle timeframes for your organization? Do you know which stakeholders to work with? If not, how can you find out the stakeholders to approach?

- Does the routine – using Align, Improve, Measure and sharing a minimum viable plan work for you? Are you already doing something similar? What can you take from this routine and adapt to your own needs?

- Does the reward apply for you? If not, what reward would there be for you to do this habit?

- What is the context currently at your organization? Is formal and informal learning already integrated into the annual planning cycle? What could be improved in how it is integrated? Are all groups doing this or are there some that you could approach to get them involved?

- What suggestions from the AUTOMATIC listing are you already using? Which ones would you start to use?

Based on the above questions, consider the habit, cue, routine, reward and context – and identify what you will do to move forward in using this habit or taking pieces of it for your own use.

Back to our story

At the beginning of this chapter, we talked about a telecommunications company and the upcoming meeting for aligning on initiatives for the year. When you read that, did you have an approach already in mind? How has reading this chapter changed your approach? In real life, the meeting went very well as the context was shared ahead of time, the group assembled understood the ask and had insight into the business. They identified that they needed to gather more input

TABLE 6.1 Make the AIM to LEARN habit AUTOMATIC

AUTOMATIC	AIM to LEARN habit …
Allow for feeling good To get it done, make it fun.	Make the planning sessions fun, and reward yourself as you get them booked and when you have the draft plans done.
Under the influence If the leader is a gem, we'll follow them.	When meeting with a reluctant stakeholder, share how you did this same session with a respected executive or peer of theirs. Ensure your IMPROVE plan includes executive sponsorship from popular and well-respected leaders.
Tip the scale If we can't see it, we often won't do it.	Share examples of planning sessions from other stakeholders to show that it's the social norm to do this process.
Ownership If it's mine, I think it's super fine.	Compliment the stakeholders on what they have achieved over the past year with their groups. Recognize their success.
Mindset As a skill set grows, our fixed mindset will decompose.	If the stakeholder is uncomfortable with the questions or the process is new to them, have a prep meeting to walk them through first so they are prepared.
Avoid losses Don't ignore a potential gain just because a loss would be a pain.	Make sure the stakeholder doesn't lose face while doing the planning – if you have to group people together make sure they complement each other's capabilities.
Towards the default To be quick, go with the default pick.	For a reluctant stakeholder, have a sample plan ready to share to help them agree with the default.
Incentives A bird in the hand is worth two in the bush.	Give yourself some short-term incentives to get the planning done.
Commitment If I say it, I better do it.	Commit to your timeframe to share the overall plan and communicate that to your stakeholders.

from regional representation so they set up a learning council – but that is a different habit that we'll hear more about in Chapter 10.

Key takeaways

- AIM (Align, Improve, Measure) is a routine that you can use to align learning to organizational initiatives.
- You can adapt the process to suit your needs and current context.
- You can make AIM to LEARN automatic by following the tips in Table 6.1 (see previous page).

References

Kahneman, D (2013) *Thinking Fast and Slow*, Anchor Canada

Kander, D (2022) 3 strategies for holding yourself accountable, *Harvard Business Review* [online] https://hbr.org/2022/02/3-strategies-for-holding-yourself-accountable (archived at https://perma.cc/D867-A3SJ)

07

Executive-led dedicated time for learning

In June 2021 the global pandemic had been with us for more than a year and it had taken its toll on everyone in many ways. Wellness and self-care became popular topics as employees were encouraged to look after themselves to avoid burnout. Organizations were feeling the effects of burnout as employees chose to leave jobs that no longer satisfied their needs in a pandemic world. For many knowledge workers, having worked from home for more than a year, they struggled to demarcate between work and home. Routines had been thrown in the air with COVID and the old habits and cues were missing from people's everyday lives.

One organization* decided to address this by announcing dedicated time for learning. Their CEO announced that the company would be encouraging learning on a particular day twice a month. On the first day dedicated to learning, executives across the organization posted that they were spending time learning that day, and they shared on social media what they were doing. The company saw a huge increase in the learning done by individuals that day. The employees saw the executives set the expectation that people had time that day to learn and the executives modelled the behaviour and shared it publicly. But what happened the next learning day? We'll return to our story later to find out more.

As Steve Turner, global head of learning and skills at a major manufacturing company, shares, he has seen learning days work in a different way. At one company, they established a particular day weekly for learning. People were encouraged to learn on Tuesdays. But a strange thing happened – people were bringing in tricky problems on Tuesdays and experimenting with new ways of doing things. At first Steve says, the leadership discouraged this work as it wasn't strictly learning, but then they saw that people were learning through the work – they were trying out things they would not have done before. They were applying what they were learning in new and innovative ways. With this in mind, the company began to encourage this behaviour as it was recognized as part of the learning process, to experiment and apply the learning (Turner, 2022).

We know that we are influenced by those around us. Whether it's trying out new ideas or following the executives' lead and spending time learning new material – we are social creatures and we look to fit in with the norms of the group in which we are included. Groups in organizations are often influenced by the leadership of the group. Executives set the tone and model the behaviour that the group follows. This is very true of learning. And this brings us to our next habit – executive-led dedicated time for learning.

Overview of the habit

This habit is a keystone habit for organizations because we know that we are social creatures and we are open to influence. We know that time is a finite resource and when we're at work, we look for cues in our environment on how to spend our time, what is valued and what is looked down upon within the organization and our team. We know that learning on the job is often invisible, so bringing to light an expectation of a time and a place for self-paced learning can have a powerful effect. By setting aside dedicated time for learning, it is a keystone habit that supports self-directed learning in an organization. Executives can help with this by creating a cue for everyone. What is an effective cue for this habit?

Cue

When an organization has decided to have executive-led dedicated time for learning, they need to do more than announce the initiative and the time allotment. To benefit from the executive influence and be sure that executives are not only setting the expectation but also modelling the behaviour, the **cue for this habit is that the executive posts publicly about learning** and what they are doing in particular. They can post at the time and day when the allocated time for learning is happening. This is key to the habit being effective and followed because it shows vulnerability on the part of the executive. They are posting that they are learning and that learning is something everyone needs to do to be more effective. While we know that lifelong learning makes sense, hearing from an executive at the time and date when learning time is set aside, it is a powerful reminder that this learning time applies to everyone, including executives, and it sends a message that this is worth your time. Employees then follow and spend time learning themselves, as they have the reminder and the cue from executives. When executives announce the time and encourage everyone to learn but do not show evidence that they themselves are following this, it sends a signal that perhaps the organization does not value learning, perhaps there are other things that the employee should be concentrating on. And we see numbers drop in this case and fewer people participate.

Routine

The **routine for this habit** is quite simple but difficult to execute consistently. Learning is one of those things that is important but not generally urgent. That's why with this habit it's important that the **executive not only sets the expectation for dedicated time for learning, they need to show employees that they are learning and the executive posts about what they are doing, each time the dedicated time comes around. Employees will then follow the expectation and spend time learning** and the organization as a whole will be promoting learning. To reinforce the learning and recognize that people are spending time learning, the organization needs to celebrate learning and share evidence of learning by encouraging social sharing about learning.

Reward

The **reward** for following this habit in this way is that **employees will feel supported in their development** – and they will be less likely to leave the organization. The organization will benefit from a more engaged and future-ready workforce. There are many benefits to learning, which the organization can gather and celebrate. This habit will allow employees the time and space to learn – and the organization can use established methods to ascertain the value of learning for their organization.

Context

With this habit in place, the context in the organization will shift the social norm around learning in the company. **It will become the social norm that learning is expected and shared.** People will feel safe to spend time learning and this will help lead to innovation and new ways of working. Context is a major factor in whether employees feel the psychological safety to spend time learning. With this habit, they will see the cue each time the dedicated time comes around. For example, if it's every third Thursday of the month, and the afternoons are for learning, they'll see the cue when the executives post publicly. By setting this example and showing their leadership, other leaders in the organization will also share about their learning. With the leadership clearly indicating that each time that dedicated time for learning arrives that they themselves are learning, the employees will feel safe to spend time learning themselves. They will feel safe to talk about what they are learning with peers. Employees will discuss their learning and reinforce what they have been learning, they will have the space to discuss their learning with others and, by doing this, conversations about how to apply the learning at work will become more common. All of these connections and conversations will support the change in context and show employees that time for learning is expected and supported.

FIGURE 7.1 The executive-led dedicated time for learning habit

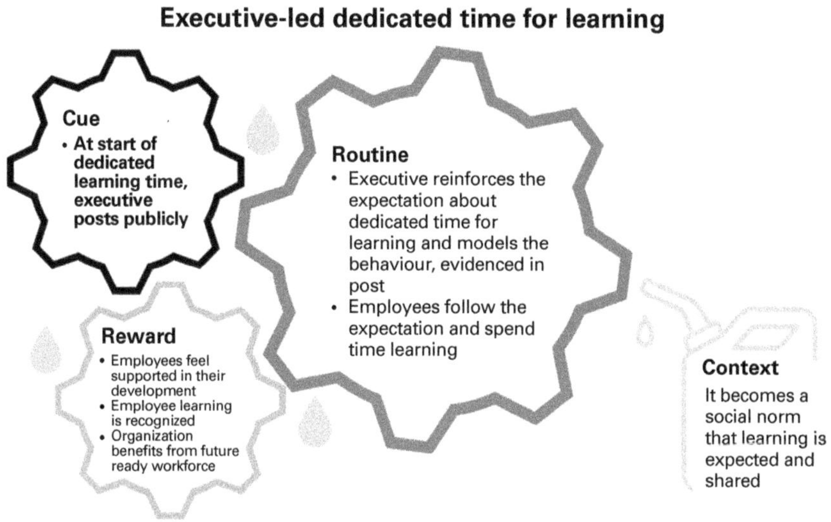

Executive-led dedicated time for learning

Cue
• At start of dedicated learning time, executive posts publicly

Routine
• Executive reinforces the expectation about dedicated time for learning and models the behaviour, evidenced in post
• Employees follow the expectation and spend time learning

Reward
• Employees feel supported in their development
• Employee learning is recognized
• Organization benefits from future ready workforce

Context
It becomes a social norm that learning is expected and shared

Measurement for the habit

To measure this habit, you can look at a few areas. As the cue hinges on the social posts of executives, you may want to track how often they are posting, if leadership is posting and how many people are looking at the posts. Since the time is being allocated for learning, you can look at systems and session attendance to see how many people are spending time in learning and what type of learning they are doing. Keep in mind they may also be learning offline through books or other areas that are not trackable in your corporate systems. Last, you can use your measures identified in AIM to LEARN to see how the time spent in learning is impacting the identified key performance indicators.

Here are the three main areas for measurement with suggestions for metrics to track:

1 Evidence of learning from social posts

   o number of executives posting

   o number of leaders posting (directors, managers, etc.)

- reach of posts – how many people viewed them?
- number of external posts
- number of internal posts or mentions
- number of employees who post
- number of business divisions with posts
- number of regions with posts

2 Time spent in learning from systems and sessions
- number of hours spent learning per learning system
- number of employees who spent time learning in learning systems
- number of teams who had employees spending time in learning systems
- number of divisions who had employees spending time in learning systems
- number of employees who reported they spend time learning outside of systems (gathered through survey or other means)

3 Influence of learning on key performance indicators (KPIs)
- results on KPIs identified in AIM to LEARN before and after dedicated time
- results on KPIs in groups who participated in dedicated learning time vs groups who did not participate in dedicated learning time
- KPIs for groups with executives who posted publicly vs groups with executives who did not post publicly

As with any measurement, you need to decide on what is available to measure and the amount of effort involved in the measurement vs the amount of gain from understanding the metrics. For example, if it would be very time-consuming to gather information about social posts across the organization, perhaps gather it for one business unit as a sample.

Make this habit AUTOMATIC

A – Allow for feeling good. For this habit, remember to make the tone of communications, especially the social posts, show a fun and exciting vibe. You want to avoid making it sound like just one more thing people need to do, another burden they need to fit in. To support keeping a fun and exciting tone, you could share sample types of posts with leadership to help them post and personalize what they are saying about how they are spending time learning.

U – Under the influence. You'll want to ensure that your most influential executives post about their learning. You can seek out the most popular and respected executives to get them posting about their learning. Their influence will go a long way in bringing others on board and changing the context for learning in the organization.

T – Tip the scale. With learning, especially self-directed individual learning, it is often hard to know what the benchmark is for how much to do and when. In many cases, there isn't obvious social proof of learning. That's why it's so important for leaders to post *each* time there is dedicated time for learning, not just the first few times.

O – Ownership. To foster a sense of community in learning and trigger the ownership bias that people have, you can give the dedicated time for learning a name. This will encourage employees to think of it as something that belongs to the organization, and by extension to themselves as employees of that organization. It will foster the tribal nature of our thinking, as in 'this is the way we do things here'. And by giving it a name, you'll also trigger the endowment effect, which tells us we overvalue things simply because they are ours.

M – Mindset. As with posting with a fun and engaging tone, another underlying message needs to be that the organization supports and celebrates a growth mindset. The executives' posts can share that they are learning and growing – that even though they are successful executives, they are continually learning and improving. This will help show that they are open to development, they expect growth, and they are not simply reinforcing the value of their existing skill set. This will help to shift people's thinking from a fixed mindset to a growth mindset.

A – Avoid losses. Managers and employees may feel a time loss as they look to follow the learning expectation and commit to the dedicated time for learning. They may feel a loss and regret having less time to focus on work aligned to the results they are responsible for. To mitigate this risk, ensure that you message the benefits of learning, and how learning will help accomplish the results they are responsible for. You can also offer short-term incentives for participating in learning, to help people overcome the sense of loss of time.

T – Towards the default. You can make it easy for people to participate by sending a calendar invite for the dedicated learning time or have each executive send a calendar invite to their group. This will make it easier for people to participate as it will be on their calendar, they may book fewer meetings, or better yet no meetings, during the dedicated learning time.

I – Incentives. People love short-term rewards. So be sure to give out randomized rewards for learning, or for posting about learning or for both. This will encourage people to participate and it will keep things fresh by being randomized. They can look for a short-term reward to help them get over any short-term loss of participating. It will also help people post who maybe wouldn't post without a quick reward right away.

C – Commitment. As you meet with executives to get them involved in the dedicated time for learning, have them share publicly about what their plan for learning is – and then follow up to encourage them to post about their learning when they do it. We tend to want to continue with our commitments – so use this to encourage executives to participate.

YOUR ACTION PLAN

As you consider this habit, and decide if you want to use it within your organization, think about how you could do that. Would the cue work in your organizational context or do you need to change it? What would the routine look like in your company? How would the rewards work in your company? And do the social norms in your company already support the context for this habit or would you be helping to move the company to a more supportive place for learning by using this habit? What suggestions from how to make it AUTOMATIC would work for your use of this habit? Consider these questions and form your own plan about this habit. What is the first step you will take to get started?

Back to our story

When we started this chapter we talked about companies that have executive-led dedicated time for learning. But what we didn't address was if there is a difference between when executives post publicly about their learning and when they do not. What we see across many companies is that when the social norm for learning is not reinforced regularly by executives through their social media posts, and their other communications, then the organization does not have as much learning happening, even when there is dedicated time for learning. Without a clear and regular signal from leadership about learning and regular mentions about it, people get the message that learning is not something that is valued and they tend to spend less time learning, and less time talking about and benefiting from their learning.

And that's exactly what happened in our story. The company's executives stopped posting about their learning on social media. While the novelty of the learning time also decreased over time, without the public cues from executives, the employees spent less time engaged in learning materials.

Key takeaways

- When executives post publicly about their learning, it shows the social norms support learning and makes learning visible for the organization.
- Leadership and employees will look to executives for how to behave – and when they see and hear about executives learning they will spend time learning themselves.
- Measurement of learning can help to look at the effectiveness of learning within the company. The executive-led dedicated time for learning will drive the learning time, and then the benefits of time spent in learning can be measured in line with your key performance indicators as set out in AIM to LEARN, making this a keystone habit for success with self-directed learning.

- The executive-led dedicated time for learning habit can be made AUTOMATIC by following the suggestions in the chapter and summarized in Table 7.1.

TABLE 7.1 Make the executive-led time for learning habit AUTOMATIC

AUTOMATIC	Executive-led time for learning habit...
Allow for feeling good To get it done, make it fun.	Make the communications fun and exciting – not a burden on people.
Under the influence If the leader is a gem, we'll follow them.	Have popular and respected executives post about the dedicated time.
Tip the scale If we can't see it, we often won't do it.	Make sure social proof is obvious – have leaders post, every time not just the first time.
Ownership If it's mine, I think it's super fine.	Give the dedicated time a name – tie it to the sense of organizational belonging.
Mindset As a skill set grows, our fixed mindset will decompose.	Ensure messaging fosters a growth mindset – and encourage executives to share what they are learning so it shows a growth mindset.
Avoid losses Don't ignore a potential gain just because a loss would be a pain.	Help managers overcome the time loss from their teams by messaging the organizational gains from learning – and give short-term incentives at the team level.
Towards the default To be quick, go with the default pick.	Create a calendar invite and send to everyone to block the time so it's on their calendar.

(continued)

TABLE 7.1 (Continued)

AUTOMATIC	Executive-led time for learning habit...
Incentives A bird in the hand is worth two in the bush.	Have periodic random rewards – for learning, for posting – for teams that learn and post.
Commitment If I say it, I better do it.	Have each leader commit publicly about what they will do and how they will do it – then follow up and have them post about what they've done.

Endnote

*This is a fictionalized story based on several real-life examples.

Reference

Turner, S (2022) Global Head of Learning and Skills [Interview] (14 April 2022)

08

Fiscal year start

At a tech company in early 2022, after a second difficult year during the pandemic, the chief revenue officer sent out a message just as the fiscal year kicked off. In the message, she empathized with the employees about the difficulties of living and working during the pandemic. She also set out the expectations for the revenue organization to learn a new selling methodology that was going to help the company achieve its objectives in 2022. Learning the methodology would be a six-hour time commitment for sessions, as well as independent work that would take more than four hours. As the sales team heard about this, they wondered how they would accomplish this together with their territory planning and regular activities at the start of the year. Let's look into the habit that this story illustrates.

Overview of the habit

This habit is called fiscal year start and it's really about the executive communication at the beginning of the fiscal year. Just as with the executive-led dedicated time for learning, this fiscal year start habit revolves around the executive communicating expectations. While a person's direct manager is an important influence on employee development, executives also play a key role. They can set the expectation and model the behaviour. With this habit in particular, the executive is sharing a key insight on important initiatives and how learning will support the achievement of the aligned objectives. With organizational attention at a premium, and employees pressed for time, a message coming from an executive at the beginning of the fiscal year will attract their attention and let them know why the initiative and supporting learning matters. Let's have a look.

Cue

The cue for this habit is the beginning of the fiscal year. This is an important temporal landmark in every company and it is often when employees hear about what the focus for the fiscal year is and what initiatives are planned to help the company achieve its goals. Many companies have formal processes and well-established communications to share the company vision and goals for the year. But something that is often missing from the executive communications at this time is learning, and this is a lost opportunity. We know from research that temporal landmarks are opportunities to change our routine or work towards new goals (Milkman, 2021). Also known as the fresh start effect, we often begin new projects and make changes at particular points – the start of a new week, the start of a new month, after a milestone birthday or the start of a new year. At these points, we often step away from the day-to-day view and consider the bigger picture, then look at our old selves and what we want for our new selves as we look at the fresh beginning on the calendar. That's why the timing of this habit is so important as it takes advantage of this temporal landmark inside the organization and for individuals.

Routine

The routine for this habit hinges on the executive. At the start of the fiscal year, the executive sends out a communication to their business unit outlining their expectations for learning as it aligns to their initiatives for the year. This can be as simple as sharing a video explaining the focus for initiatives and what key skills will be needed.

For example, a Chief Information Officer (CIO) could share a video explaining how the information technology group will support the company's focus on being customer-centric and accessible. The CIO could share how the key skills needed will be cloud, agile and accessible design, and how learning will align to this and where and how it will be made available. By hearing this from the CIO, the information technology group will see how the skills align to what they need to get done, and they'll hear from their CIO about the importance of spending time on this. If the AIM to LEARN (Chapter 6) habit is already in use, then the materials will be available to support this learning, as it was discussed during the planning phase in the organization and learning was aligned and the measurement expectations set. If the executive-driven time for learning is already in use, then employees will have information, not just on what to learn about, but when to learn. And the division-wide message at the start of the fiscal year will reinforce the social norm of learning and show employees how their learning aligns to this year's initiatives, reinforcing why it's worth their time.

Reward

The reward for this habit is that the executive has demonstrated their support for learning, which can lead to higher engagement scores and stronger employee retention in their group. The longer-term benefit is that this messaging will **set up the group for success to deliver on the initiatives** as they already know what learning is expected and needed in order to deliver their part in the organizational initiatives. The team will be better prepared to support the initiatives as they know what learning is aligned and expected so they can focus their time there.

Context

The context for this habit is that learning is aligned to the business and it is expected and shared by executives. By communicating in this way, executives will show that they understand how learning will support key initiatives and they share this information explicitly with their group, showing their support for learning. All of this supports a context where learning is part of the social norms of the group.

FIGURE 8.1   Fiscal year start habit

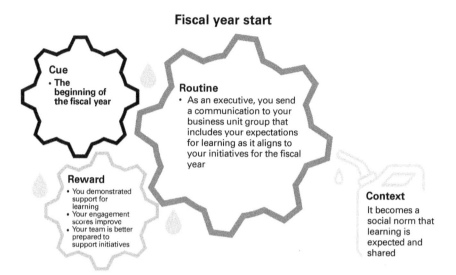

Measurement for the habit

You can measure this habit in a few different ways. You can look at the evidence of executives sending communications. You can look at the evidence of employee engagement scores and the preparedness of teams to work on initiatives.

Specifically, here are some sample measurements you can consider using:

1 Executive posting

  ○ number of executives who sent communications at fiscal year start to entire division

  ○ number of executives who sent communications that included expectations for learning

  ○ open rate or views on the communications sent by executives

  ○ percentage of the organization who received a communication from an executive with learning expectations

  ○ number of days/weeks after the fiscal year start that a communication was sent

2 Employee engagement

- o employee engagement score for groups that received a communication vs groups that did not
- o employee engagement score before the communication and after the communication
- o attrition rate for groups that received a communication vs groups that did not

3 Team preparedness

- o feedback from managers on team's skills and abilities, after receiving communication and spending time on aligned learning
- o competency or skill assessments for groups who received a communication and their competency rating or learning assessment results one quarter after communication

These measures won't be all available to you and you don't need to use all of them to get a picture of how the habit is working. Select the ones that you can access and which will provide you with enough data to use as feedback on the habit's effectiveness and ubiquity.

Make this habit AUTOMATIC

A – Allow for feeling good. Everyone benefits when something is more fun – even executives. They can make this process more fun by having a little friendly challenge or competition to get their messages out. Something like the last one to send their message has to buy the others a forfeit prize – and this can be something appropriate for the culture of the organization. If appropriate, and depending on the size of the company, the CEO may even get involved and recognize those who get their messages out.

U – Under the influence. In addition to the CEO being involved recognizing those who have sent their messages out, the CEO could also lead by example in sending his or her own message and by setting the expectation of when the messages need to be sent out.

T – **Tip the scale.** The communication from the executive can be just the start. You can make learning and learning expectations more visible by following up with additional postings and communications to reinforce the messaging, making the whole process more visible and increasing the expectation of support for learning.

O – **Ownership.** Make sure the messaging reinforces the company initiatives and how this learning will help achieve the goals that everyone owns. This will help employees see why they would want to spend time on this learning in particular and how it shows their membership in the company group.

M – **Mindset.** This type of messaging from an executive is another great opportunity for them to share what their own learning plans are – this will show that development is expected and supported and that the executive embraces a growth mindset.

A – **Avoid losses.** Encourage the executives to focus on the positives of the initiatives and the aligned learning and how they help the company succeed. Share sample messages with a positive tone to share how to set the right context for the message to encourage employees.

T – **Towards the default.** Make it easy for employees to follow the expectation set out. After the message is sent, add the employees to learning paths with aligned materials. If you've followed the AIM to LEARN habit, you will have this material ready to go – and you can add all employees so that they can click and learn easily, or get scheduled in available sessions. If the system you're using also has the ability to email the learners, you can have the link sent out to them so they can easily click to get started while the messaging is fresh.

I – **Incentives.** Look for ways to incorporate short-term incentives into the messaging and follow-up. If possible, offer a quick thank you or incentive to executives who send out communications, and have periodic rewards for employees who are doing aligned learning. You could also have them share their stories so others can hear how they are learning.

C – **Commitment.** Tie in learning plans or development plans to this messaging, so that employees can think about what their own plan is, write it down and then share that with their manager. This will help them to commit to the action and work out how they will get around any obstacles that may appear as they work on this learning aligned to initiatives.

YOUR ACTION PLAN

If you're responsible for the learning function in the organization, and you're considering using this habit, think through the executives and your stakeholders. Who would participate in this? When is your fiscal year start? Did you follow the AIM to LEARN habit or another method to ensure you have aligned learning ready and available? What measurements do you have access to and which ones will you use? Would you consider a phased approach for this with some executives starting it, you analyse the results and then share the success with other groups to help them get onboard?

You'll need to consider what the cue for this type of messaging would be in your organization. You'll want to consider who would send messages and what your plan is for making this habit AUTOMATIC. Identify what your first step is to get started and begin there.

Back to our story

What happened at that tech company when the Chief Revenue Officer shared that messaging at the start of the fiscal year? The revenue organization spent the time in the learning sessions, they did the individual work and the leaders reinforced the need to do the work. The methodology was integrated into how people talked about deals and used within the systems for tracking sales. Despite a challenging economic time, the company had a strong first half, and much of that can be attributed to the alignment within the revenue organization about the new methodology and applying it within accounts.[*]

Key takeaways

- Executives are key influencers in organizations and can articulate the link from learning to aligned initiatives and anticipated business results.

- The fiscal year start is an important temporal landmark within organizations.
- Employees are more willing to learn when they know how the learning aligns to the results on which they are being measured.

TABLE 8.1 Make the fiscal year start habit AUTOMATIC

AUTOMATIC	Fiscal year start habit …
Allow for feeling good To get it done, make it fun.	Encourage executives to challenge each other in getting messages out – they can have an informal competition to get their messages out.
Under the influence If the leader is a gem, we'll follow them.	Ask the CEO to send a message including an expectation for when executives will message their groups.
Tip the scale If we can't see it, we often won't do it.	Encourage more communication – through postings or collaboration tools – to reinforce the executives' message and remind employees about the expectation.
Ownership If it's mine, I think it's super fine.	If the initiatives have names used in the organization, include those names in the messaging to include a sense of ownership. Even better, name the learning with an organization-specific moniker.
Mindset As a skill set grows, our fixed mindset will decompose.	Ask the executive to include in their message what their own plan for learning is, so that employees see their growth mindset in action.
Avoid losses Don't ignore a potential gain just because a loss would be a pain.	Encourage the executive to focus on the positives of achieving the initiatives and the aligned learning.

(continued)

TABLE 8.1 (Continued)

AUTOMATIC	Fiscal year start habit …
Towards the default To be quick, go with the default pick.	After the executive sends the communication, follow up by adding all employees to an aligned learning path or sending a calendar invite for learning time with links to aligned sessions or content.
Incentives A bird in the hand is worth two in the bush.	Reward the executives for sending the communication and share periodic rewards with employees as they work on aligned learning.
Commitment If I say it, I better do it.	Ask the executive to include a link to a learning plan or development plan for employees with the ask that each employee commit to their own learning plan and share it with their manager.

Endnote

*This is a fictionalized story based on several real-world examples.

Reference

Milkman, K (2021) *How to Change: The science of getting from where you are to where you want to be*, Portfolio Penguin, New York

09

Company-wide meetings

At a large company a few years ago, the employees gathered for a company-wide meeting. The agenda was well planned and included updates on the company initiatives, strategy and forecast. A number of executives spoke and recognized outstanding contributions by employees. But the meeting included something different to their regular updates, and it caused a ripple effect. We'll hear more about this later but first let's dive into our next habit.

Overview of the habit

The company-wide meeting is a great opportunity to include learning habits. It's a good opportunity for a learning habit because the company-wide meeting is an opportunity to communicate across the organization, important updates are shared and employees are recognized. It can be powerful social proof of learning if learning is highlighted and accomplishments are recognized and celebrated. So how does this habit break down?

Cue

When it's time to plan a company-wide meeting, that's the cue for this habit. Company-wide meetings involve a lot of preparation and alignment on the agenda, so this is when your stakeholders can be key in helping to get you involved in the company-wide meeting. If you're following the AIM to LEARN habit and if you have also included the executive-led dedicated time for learning, then you will already know how learning aligns to the company's initiatives and which KPIs you are looking to impact. You will already know which stakeholders to speak with, and if you're measuring the two habits, you will have results to share about learning in the organization. If you're not yet using AIM to LEARN or executive-led dedicated time for learning, you can still use the company-wide meeting as an opportunity to highlight relevant learning and share results. As you start with this habit, it may be more informal, but just getting learning on the agenda and starting small can help to bring attention and focus to learning in the organization, in support of business results.

Routine

For this habit, the routine is that you would add an item to the agenda to highlight learning. This could take the form of having an employee briefly share a recent learning-related accomplishment, like an interesting course and how they applied the learning; or a recent certification and how it helped their career path. You could also share overall learning accomplishments or rewards for learning; or highlight what a team has recently done with learning and how it helped their results. You could have an executive share a recent learning activity and what they gained from it. The point of the routine is to make learning visible and celebrated. We know from research that people are more likely to do something if they hear about someone like them who has done something similar (Cialdini, 2021). We're influenced by peers and when we see someone in similar circumstances to ourselves accomplish something, we are more likely to try it ourselves and believe that we can accomplish it as well (Cialdini, 2021).

In addition, if the story shared is from a learning offering that others in the company have access to, by highlighting the specific offering in the company-wide meeting, we can benefit from the decision heuristic that many people use, which is to choose something because others have chosen it. Basically, to make faster decisions, we decide that if others have chosen it, it is most likely that it's good for us as well, and we skip doing a deep dive into whether it is the best choice for us in particular (Cialdini, 2021).

Reward

The reward for this habit is that you highlight learning in the organization and share stories that people can relate to, about how learning is helping. This **increases the social proof of learning in the company and helps to support the expectation and behaviour of learning habits,** and with that, all the benefits that come with learning. If you've also followed AIM to LEARN then much of the learning happening will support company initiatives and results. In addition, a short-term benefit is that employees receive recognition and rewards for learning, which helps to give them incentives to continue, and gives incentives to those seeing the rewards and recognition, to start or continue learning activities themselves.

Context

By highlighting learning and sharing relatable stories at company-wide meetings, you help to shift the context to make learning part of the way things are done. **This habit supports the social norm of learning within the organization.** If you vary the stories at each meeting to highlight individual contributors, leaders and teams you'll showcase a different example each time with stories that are relatable at various levels and for various purposes. This will help to embed the social norm of learning across the levels of your organization.

In addition, by including a variety of stories interspersed with rewards and recognition, you'll keep it fresh each time and this will garner more attention from your employees. If the rewards are sporadically shared and more randomized, this will help to make them unexpected and encourage others to follow. We know from research that uncertain rewards are more desirable than predictable rewards (Wood, 2019).

FIGURE 9.1 Company-wide meetings habit

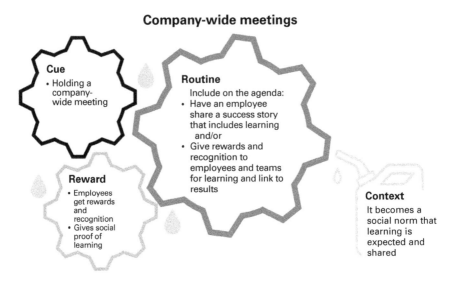

Company-wide meetings

Cue
- Holding a company-wide meeting

Routine
Include on the agenda:
- Have an employee share a success story that includes learning and/or
- Give rewards and recognition to employees and teams for learning and link to results

Reward
- Employees get rewards and recognition
- Gives social proof of learning

Context
It becomes a social norm that learning is expected and shared

Measurement for the habit

For the company-wide meetings learning habit, you can measure the habit and its impact in various ways:

- number of company-wide meetings that included learning highlights on agenda

- number of company-wide meetings that included learning highlights on agenda – sorted by which roles and which teams highlighted

- number of times executives shared learning stories in company meetings

- number of times teams shared or were highlighted for learning stories in company meetings

- number of time rewards or recognition included in company-wide meetings

- use of learning before a company-wide meeting and use of learning after a company-wide meeting

- use of learning material mentioned in company-wide meeting before and after meeting
- employee engagement scores before and after using this company-wide learning habit

Make this habit AUTOMATIC

A – Allow for feeling good. When adding learning to the company-wide meeting agenda, make it fun. Share uplifting stories, share where things went wrong and include humour in sharing the stories. When encouraging employees to share their stories, make it easy for them to do it by giving them coaching or examples. If you're giving rewards and recognition, make some of the awards light-hearted and fun. By making this part of the meeting fun you will encourage your employees and help to put those who are sharing at ease.

U – Under the influence. To use influence for the habit, have a popular executive share a learning story or learning ideas in the company-wide meeting. As with other learning habits, people are influenced by who they hear from. You can also use influence by having employees share their stories so that people relate to the story and see others like them who have achieved results.

T – Tip the scale. We want to hear from others like us so in your planning for company-wide meetings, be sure to vary which teams and roles' stories are highlighted. You want to make the learning examples resonate with your audience, so over time, as you include learning on the agenda, be sure to have highlighted stories from across the breadth and depth of the teams and roles at your company.

O – Ownership. You can foster a sense of ownership of this habit by giving the learning agenda item a name. You can still vary what agenda item about learning is shared – if it's recognition, reward, an individual story or an item shared by an executive – but it would all be under the same agenda item name. By branding the agenda item, it develops the feeling that this is something we do at our company and this is how we do it here in particular. Giving the item a name will also act as a cue to include it in every meeting and help to set the expectation among employees that this item will be covered at every company-wide meeting.

M – Mindset. When you help team members and executives prepare for sharing their learning stories make sure they use growth mindset wording. You'll want to help the stories foster a growth mindset across the audience. When sharing learning data, use it to highlight progress and how learning is developing people. You wouldn't want to share learning data in a way that feels like it is an inspection. Share success stories and examples of growth, rather than sharing data across the organization and identifying which groups are not keeping up.

A – Avoid losses. Similar to fostering a growth mindset, you'll want to ensure that stories shared are done so by employees who feel supported and comfortable to share their story. If they perceive they will lose anything by sharing, they will be more hesitant to share. When working with them in prep, ensure they clearly know the gain for themselves in sharing, and that they know they are helping others to also learn. Vary who shares their stories as well so that you have a diverse set of individuals over time that share, so that everyone can recognize themselves in the stories.

T – Towards the default. To make it easy to include learning on the agenda, make it part of the standard agenda, so that it's the default to include learning rather than something to add on sometimes. This is where naming the agenda item, with something that fosters a sense of ownership, will also come in handy – as then the agenda can include this standard name, rather than a specifically named individual item that covers learning.

I – Incentives. You can share rewards for learning. However, keep it randomized so that rewards or prizes are not shared every time, but done sporadically, so that you get the benefit of randomized awards and you keep attention on the learning section of the agenda. Also, by sharing incentives in the meeting, you'll give people short-term incentives for learning, since often the benefits of investing time in learning are longer-term career related benefits that may not be as appealing immediately as a quick short-term prize.

C – Commitment. As part of the regular agenda item covering learning, you can have employees or executives share their learning goals. This will have a two-fold benefit – people will see others committing to a path and this may make them more likely to commit to a learning path themselves. And second, the person committing publicly to a learning path will be more likely to follow through on it, once they have stated their intention publicly.

YOUR ACTION PLAN

Decide on how you could use this habit in your organization. Here are some considerations as you look to build your action plan:

- Is there a company-wide meeting and how would you get a learning agenda item added?
- Who would you need to speak with to make that happen?
- What could you call the agenda item?
- How will you explain the need for speaking about learning in the company wide meeting?
- Who could you ask to share stories?
- What type of learning successes could people share?
- How would you identify different roles and teams in order to gain depth and breadth in the learning stories shared?
- Do you currently have rewards or quick prizes for learning? What are they?
- If you don't have them, could rewards or prizes be implemented?
- Would you consider having non-monetary prizes like lunch with an executive or coffee with the CEO?
- What other kinds of prizes could you have?
- Are there any restrictions on prizes for different locations of the company?
- Is the company meeting a global event?
- How far in advance would you need to plan in order to have an item added to the agenda?

Consider these questions and formulate a plan for how you could use this habit in your company. Where will you start? What's the next action that you could do to begin?

Back to our story

At the beginning of this chapter we heard about an organization where the company meeting included a new agenda item that caused a ripple effect.* As you may have guessed by now, that agenda item was learning. An executive shared their recent result on an assessment that was part of the company's learning offering. The results were shared with growth mindset language and the executive was popular in the company. The type of assessment the executive shared was available to everyone in the company through their corporate learning system.

After the company-wide meeting, people who had been hesitant to do an assessment suddenly logged onto the system and tried them out. The assessment enabled employees to get their own personalized path for learning and many employees continued – they didn't just take the assessment, they did some of the suggested learning.

When the next company meeting came around, this time instead of having an executive share their learning story, they had an individual contributor speak about how the learning made a difference to them personally in their role. The company again saw an increase in usage as more people decided that if others were doing this, they could too. Over time, the company-wide meetings continued to highlight learning and the use of learning resources for continuous learning kept growing at the company.

Key takeaways

- Company-wide meetings are often an established habit in organizations, you can add learning to embed learning in the social norms of the organization

TABLE 9.1 Make the company-wide meetings habit AUTOMATIC

AUTOMATIC	Company-wide meetings habit ...
Allow for feeling good To get it done, make it fun.	Make the inclusion of learning fun with light-hearted terms and learning.

(continued)

TABLE 9.1 (Continued)

AUTOMATIC	Company-wide meetings habit ...
Under the influence If the leader is a gem, we'll follow them.	Have a popular executive share learning ideas.
Tip the scale If we can't see it, we often won't do it.	Make sure to highlight different teams each time.
Ownership If it's mine, I think it's super fine.	Give the learning agenda item a name – maybe something tied to your existing corporate values – so that there is a sense of ownership of the learning.
Mindset As a skill set grows, our fixed mindset will decompose.	Ensure the learning is shared using growth mindset feedback and that data is shared for learning not inspection.
Avoid losses Don't ignore a potential gain just because a loss would be a pain.	Share positive results and share negative results as a learning mechanism not inspection.
Towards the default To be quick, go with the default pick.	Make learning part of the default agenda.
Incentives A bird in the hand is worth two in the bush.	Share spot prizes in the company wide meeting – for random acts of learning – and keep people guessing about what the qualifiers will be.
Commitment If I say it, I better do it.	Have managers or executives share their learning goals.

Endnote

*This is a fictionalized story based on several real-life examples.

References

Cialdini, R B (2021) *Influence: The psychology of persuasion: New and expanded*, Harper Business, New York

Wood, W (2019) *Good Habits, Bad Habits: The science of making positive changes that stick*, Farrar, Straus and Giroux, New York

10

Learning council

At a financial services company[*] in 2015, they needed to gather input about learning needs, align their learning purchases to benefit from economies of scale and drive learning engagement throughout the global organization. To gain perspective and engage stakeholders across the geographies, they formed a learning council and had leaders from each global group join the council.

During the kick-off call, the VP of Learning and Development laid out what the purpose of the council was, how they would help share what skills were needed in their groups and how they could get resources to build those skills.

The central learning group had purchased a number of learning offerings that the regional geographies could then use to meet learning needs in their own groups, without each group purchasing solutions separately at higher individual costs. The council helped articulate what their groups needed for skills to support the organization's strategic priorities. The company was able to drive engagement in learning solutions, standardize how reporting was done on learning to examine results, and enable more people to be aware of the learning offerings and access them, all at a lower cost than if the council and the central learning group had not worked together.

But a few years later, there was no council in existence and each group was purchasing their own learning offerings at a higher overall cost. What had gone wrong? Let's look at our next habit – learning councils.

Overview of the habit

While at first it may seem that a learning council isn't a habit at all, the act of the learning council meeting and being effective is a learning habit for organizations. It can support learning in the organization and in large organizations in particular, when the learning council gets to the level of being a habit, it can help foster effective learning across the organization. You can name it something less formal, depending on your organization, such as a champion or ambassador group. When combined with AIM to LEARN and dedicated time for learning, the learning council can help ensure that each region's needs are represented in the planning cycle and in the learning opportunities within the organization. This in turn can help the organization and individuals achieve the goals they set out for learning and key performance indicators. So what exactly does a learning council look like as a habit?

Cue

The cue for the learning council is a quarterly invite for a meeting. Typically, the council would be made up of representatives from each business unit or region. The representatives would ideally be from the business in a leadership role and be familiar with their unit's key initiatives and performance metrics (Harper, 2022). The leader of the business unit would likely have asked the person to represent them on the learning council. The council could have meetings more regularly than quarterly, the cadence of the meetings can be adjusted based on the organizational needs and culture, but at a minimum they would meet quarterly to align with planning and results monitoring.

Routine

The routine for this habit is that during the meeting, updates would be shared with the group about the learning offerings that are available, evidence of learning engagement and learning habits, what results are happening with learning and impact on key performance indicators. Next **the learning leads can share what's happening in their groups** and have the opportunity to learn from each other. Finally, **tools and resources can be shared** to help foster learning engagement and results in the business units; and expectations can be reinforced about what the leads are expected to do in their business units and why they would want to foster learning habits.

Reward

The reward for running a learning council in this manner with quarterly meetings is that the central group has a conduit to share resources and updates with each regional group. The regional groups have a conduit to learn from each other and see that learning is supported and what outcomes are in evidence. Finally, the leads can be recognized and rewarded for their personal involvement in the council by the clear expectations set and their opportunity to network and share back insight with the leader of their business unit. In this way, **the council provides social support for learning; and leads are supported and recognized for their participation.**

FIGURE 10.1 Learning council habit

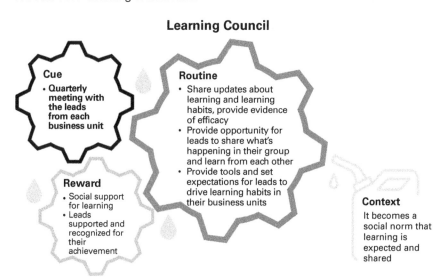

Learning Council

Cue
• Quarterly meeting with the leads from each business unit

Routine
• Share updates about learning and learning habits, provide evidence of efficacy
• Provide opportunity for leads to share what's happening in their group and learn from each other
• Provide tools and set expectations for leads to drive learning habits in their business units

Reward
• Social support for learning
• Leads supported and recognized for their achievement

Context
It becomes a social norm that learning is expected and shared

Context

The context for this habit is that the social norm for learning is spread across the organization and throughout the business units. With each region or business unit represented, and with results and outcomes regularly shared, there is ample evidence of learning in the organization and it becomes the default way of working.

Measurement for the habit

To measure this habit and determine if you are on track, here are some suggested metrics:

- number of learning council meetings booked
- number of learning council meetings cancelled
- number of learning council meetings rebooked
- percentage of invitees who attend learning council meetings (if this trends too low, look at the reward for attending/participating, or the mix of representatives)
- percentage of invitees who share updates from their groups
- percentage of invitees who use the materials shared to foster learning in their groups
- evidence of alignment to key performance indicators across regions/business units
- evidence of learning engagement with materials aligned to key performance indicators across regions/business units
- results on key performance indicators across business units for those with learning engagement/participation on council vs results on key performance indicators across business units for those without learning engagement and/or participation on council
- feedback from council members on benefits from participating for their groups and for themselves

Make this habit AUTOMATIC

A – Allow for feeling good. When designing the learning council meetings, make them collaborative, and provide opportunities for members to build connections. Too often we try to fit in as much information as possible and forget that meetings are also opportunities to connect and collaborate. For a learning council in particular, the meetings need to be collaborative to benefit from the members participation, and they need to be enjoyable as much as possible, so that members will attend and participate. You may be inclined to share a lot of information and slides, but if that's the case, the members may just decide they can skip and say they will review the slides and/or recording later.

U – Under the influence. To gather members for the council, be cognisant of who asks them to participate and who follows up with them about their participation. If possible, have the leader of their region or business unit ask them to participate. When they ask them, they should also include the why behind the ask and how participation will help the business unit/region and what the benefits are for the individual in participating. You may want to consider making participation for a set term, so people know when they are expected to start and stop participating. In addition, you could consider having the leaders send thank yous to the participants on an annual basis to recognize their work on the council and thank them for the impact they are having in fostering learning throughout the organization.

T – Tip the scale. During the learning council meetings, have each member share what is happening in their groups and how they are using the resources provided to foster continuous learning in their groups. You could provide space for each member to share their perspective supported with the statistics or anecdotes about continuous learning that they want to highlight with the group. This will give each member the opportunity to hear what's working or not working with other groups and it will make what's happening in each group visible.

O – Ownership. The group will benefit from sharing resources, ideas and encouraging learning habits in the learning council forum.

Encourage each member to use resources and ideas shared in a way that makes sense for their group. They are representing their region and they can localize and tweak the ideas and resources shared to fit their group. They can foster a sense of ownership for their use of the materials, and, by localizing them, their groups will benefit from resources and messaging that suits their geography and group.

M – Mindset. It can be challenging to encourage continuous learning with a growth mindset focus. Some members may tend to use learning data for inspection or put a lot of requirements for approvals in front of learning that discourage continuous learning and learning habits in their groups. This is where the group sharing can help as well – highlighting and reinforcing stories that show a growth mindset and development outlook.

A – Avoid losses. In asking people to participate as members in the learning council, you are asking them to give their time and attention to the council, and they will need to spend less time and attention on other areas. This can be perceived as a loss of time and attention for projects that they are involved in or key performance indicators they are responsible for. So make the why behind participating very clear, reinforce the purpose of the group, and let members know how they will benefit from participating. As mentioned earlier, you can make the participation on the council term-based, so people know how long they are committing for as well as the benefits to their participation.

T – Towards the default. While members may be encouraged to own the materials and resources shared and adjust them to fit their audience, you also want to make it easy to use the materials. Have templates and messaging ready and written so that members can cut and paste, adjust as needed and share with their groups. Sharing templates and materials in this way will be much more likely to be used, rather than expecting members to create their own materials.

I – Incentives. Have a contest or rewards for the members of the learning council themselves. You could have spot prizes for sharing success stories or learning statistics. You could recognize members for work they have done in their groups. You could also have executives periodically join the council and recognize the work everyone is doing. Having periodic rewards and short-term incentives will help keep members engaged.

C – Commitment. Provide opportunities for the learning council members to share what they are doing both on the council but also to let their region or business unit know what they can expect from the learning council and that person's participation. This will give the member recognition for their work and also foster commitment to continue with the plans they have shared. For example, you could have members record a short 30-second video highlighting what the plan for the year is, and then leaders could share this with the region at a town hall. The learning council members would get recognition and the region or group would know what to expect from the council.

YOUR ACTION PLAN

If your role involves managing learning in the organization, as you consider making a learning council a habit, consider these questions to formulate your action plan:

- Is there already a learning council in existence? If so, does it have a cue, routine and reward similar to what is suggested here?

- If there isn't currently a learning council, how would you establish one? Who would be effective members and how would being on a council help them? Would your leadership be in support of a learning council?

- Who would lead the learning council? How often would they meet? What tweaks would you make to the suggested agenda to make it more effective and automatic?

- What resources would you share with the learning council? Are there a variety of geographies that would need to be represented?

- If you want to move forward with a learning council, what will be your one next step to get started?

Back to our story

Let's revisit our financial services company and their learning council, which we first heard about at the beginning of the chapter. Why was the learning council gone after a few years? Despite the importance of the learning council's work, two main things caused the council to collapse.

First, each member of the council was appointed by their leadership without a clear expectation set for their participation or a clear understanding of what was in it for the council member for participating. It was important work to represent their geography on the council and bring the learning insight and best practices back to their groups, but the work was not recognized or rewarded. This meant the council member did not benefit from doing the work, but they could be perceived negatively if they didn't represent their group. With this in mind, many council members slowly stopped participating or looked for opportunities to leave the council, and they were often not replaced as it was difficult to find others to participate.

Second, some of the representatives on the council were not from the business, they were regional HR or L&D partners. This compounded the problem of participation seen from the first issue as the business representatives thought it was outside the scope of their role to be on the council, and they saw it as an HR role. With limited business participation, the council struggled to be in touch with the needs of the business, despite the best efforts of the HR and L&D partners. Eventually, the council disbanded altogether and the learning and development group struggled to get input from the regional geographies. The learning offerings became more centralized and there was less engagement in learning globally.

Perhaps if the organization had made the council's work more visible and rewarding for those from the business, and if they had looked to integrate AUTOMATIC into the design, they could have continued to benefit from the council and its impact on global reach and representation for learning in the company. Ultimately, the learning council has to be useful for the organization and for the individuals participating or it won't be worthwhile for everyone's time and attention.

Key takeaways

- A learning council is a way to get input and share resources across a large number of business units and/or global audience.
- To gain buy-in for participation on the council, make the why clear both for why it benefits the group and why it benefits the individual on the council.
- Consider making participation on the council term-based so that members know how long they are signing up for.
- Consider having executives recognize the work of the council – through periodic involvement in the meetings and through thank you letters at the end of members' terms or annually.
- Use the council to share resources and hear from each group about what is working and what is not working.

TABLE 10.1 Make the learning council habit AUTOMATIC

AUTOMATIC	Learning Council habit...
Allow for feeling good To get it done, make it fun.	Make the meetings collaborative and enjoyable – so members want to show up.
Under the influence If the leader is a gem, we'll follow them.	Have a well-liked executive invite members to be on the council.
Tip the scale If we can't see it, we often won't do it.	Ensure each meeting has an opportunity for a member to share what they are doing in their groups – so others can see what other groups are doing and learn from their peers.
Ownership If it's mine, I think it's super fine.	Encourage each member to make the learning habits and resources their own – fit for their business unit.

(continued)

TABLE 10.1 (Continued)

AUTOMATIC	Learning Council habit...
Mindset As a skill set grows, our fixed mindset will decompose.	Ensure all messaging focuses on a growth mindset – if some members are micro-managing learning or putting obstacles in the way make sure that doesn't continue.
Avoid losses Don't ignore a potential gain just because a loss would be a pain.	Make sure the time involved in the council is beneficial and members see what they are personally getting out of it.
Towards the default To be quick, go with the default pick.	Have default materials that learning council members can easily use – messaging they can cut and paste, adjust as needed and share.
Incentives A bird in the hand is worth two in the bush.	Have a contest or award prizes to the learning council members for their work and help – use existing employee recognition or give company swag.
Commitment If I say it, I better do it.	Make sure learning council members can share what their plans are – publicly – in a way that gives them credit for their work and commitment.

Endnote

*This is a fictionalized story based on several real-life examples.

Reference

Harper, C (2022) Director, Leadership, Learning and Development (retired) Learning habits in organizations [Interview] (29 April 2022)

PART THREE

Team habits

11

Quarterly business reviews and follow-ups

There was a team that had regular quarterly business reviews (QBR). Every quarter they would get together and review what went well, what could go better and what questions they had. It was a great use of everyone's time and also provided a connection and reflection point for the team. But something was missing, something wasn't happening, which meant the team wasn't set up to fully deliver on their key performance indicators. What was that one thing?

If we look at Amazon, they do something different that helps to operationalize changes. When they want to make a change, they don't rely on good intentions, instead they recognize that in order to effect change, they need to create a tool, drive adoption and inspect the results – sort of sounds like they want to make things a habit, doesn't it? They have a concept that helps with this – when they want something to change or something to be adopted by the business, they create a mechanism (Amazon Web Services, 2022).

A mechanism is the formalization of the implementation intentions for something new. Things like adding an item to a standard agenda create a mechanism to ensure that something is covered in a meeting. How does the concept of a mechanism apply to QBRs and follow-ups? We'll come back to that later, but first let's look at this habit.

Overview of the habit

The QBR and follow-up is already a habit for many teams and organizations. If your team isn't already holding QBRs, you should consider them as they are a strong method to review what's happened in the last quarter, discuss what needs to happen in the next quarter, and learn from each other about what's going well and what may work to make things better. As they occur quarterly, and they bring the team together to reflect on the past three months and get ready for the next three months, they are an opportune time to include learning in the discussion. The QBR is an opportunity to discuss resources that can help the team for the next quarter, and review resources that helped in the previous quarters. To reinforce this learning discussion, this habit includes the manager sending a follow-up note to the team after the QBR to reinforce to the team which learning resources they should focus on to help them achieve their key performance indicators for the quarter.

Cue

The cue for this habit is the team's QBR. If this isn't already an established habit, then setting out a quarterly calendar placeholder for the QBR can help to routinize holding a team QBR. As it can be challenging to find time on everyone's calendar for the QBR, if you're the manager, you could put a placeholder on your calendar to remind yourself to book the QBR and then reach out to the team and check schedules to get a time that works. Then the meeting is the cue for this habit.

Routine

The routine for the QBR includes time for each team member to **share what went well last quarter, reflect on what could go better and plan for the next quarter, including learning resources.** With the manager also participating to share the same items from the overall team perspective, this gives the team insight into leadership's expectations for the next quarter. The second component of the routine is **that the manager sends a follow-up to reinforce the key points from the QBR, including the learning resources** discussed that will support achieving the key performance indicators for the new quarter. This routine provides a reflection point for the team to come together, learn from each other and prepare for the next quarter.

Reward

The reward in completing this habit quarterly is that **your team is better prepared to achieve their key performance indicators.** As a manager, you will have demonstrated your support of your team's development, which may also lead to better engagement scores on your employee survey results, if your organization has one. You will also be encouraging the context that learning is part of the social norms of your team and that learning is supported.

Context

The context for this habit is that QBRs are standard and that learning is embedded in this standard behaviour and is supported by management, and reinforced after the QBR. If you already have QBRs occurring for your team, then this habit of including learning and following up about the learning, will support the **social norm of learning** on your team and show that learning helps **support business results.**

Measurement for the habit

There are a variety of measurements that can be used to measure the use of this habit in a team. Some of these measures may already be in use in your organization, and some are easy to start tracking. Whether you're doing this on an organizational level or whether you are looking to check your team's use of this habit, here are some suggested

FIGURE 11.1 Quarterly business reviews and follow-ups habit

Quarterly Business Reviews & Follow-Ups

Cue
• Quarterly business review meeting for team

Routine
• Include space for reflection, planning and learning on the agenda
• Post QBR, send a reminder to your team to engage in learning material that supports the team's quarterly key performance indicators

Reward
• Your team is better prepared to acheive key performance indicators
• You support your team's development

Context
It becomes a social norm that learning supports business results

measurements that you can use to set a target and then track against to ensure you are assessing the level of use and impact of this habit.

- number of QBRs held with team
- number of QBRs held with team that followed suggested routine
- number of reminders sent after QBRs
- percentage of QBRs where manager sends a reminder afterwards
- percentage achievement of key performance indicators
- percentage increase on engagement scores for the team
- percentage increase on engagement scores specific to manager supporting development for the team
- number of courses/assessments completed per quarter per team member
- number of courses/assessments that are aligned to key performance indicators, completed per quarter per team member
- average amount of time spent in courses or assessments per quarter per team member

Make this habit AUTOMATIC

A – Allow for feeling good. As a manager leading a QBR, remember that the QBR is an opportunity to connect and reflect as a team, so include some fun to foster connection. Rather than diving right into the business content, consider including an icebreaker or activity that is fun and engaging for the team. It doesn't have to be costly or time-consuming, for example, just starting with a little trivia challenge can set the stage.

U – Under the influence. After the QBR and the follow-up message, it's great to reinforce the follow-up in a team meeting. As a manager, you can have a lot of influence on your team by sharing your own learning during the quarter and what learning resources you're finding helpful to support the team's work to achieve their key performance indicators. Including this in a team meeting and sharing your own example can keep the takeaways from the QBR salient and encourage your team to apply themselves to the learning resources they need for the quarter.

T – Tip the scale. To keep learning visible and shared, encourage team members to share how their learning is going during the quarter. Team members can share what they have found useful, new material they've found applicable and how it has helped them in the work they're doing aligned to key performance indicators. This will not only reinforce how learning is aligned to business goals, but it will show team members that others are actively engaged in learning on an ongoing basis throughout the quarter, which supports the social norm of learning.

O – Ownership. To build a sense of ownership around the quarter's learning initiative, give it a name or a theme. By using a name and changing the theme every quarter, it will foster a sense of ownership on the team that 'this is how our team learns together', and by keeping this unique to your team, it will further increase the proprietary sense of learning for the team.

M – Mindset. Reflecting on the previous quarter and discussing plans during the QBR for the next quarter, combined with learning resources, will foster a growth mindset for the group. They will be learning together, discussing the efforts to achieve goals and recognizing that there are learning opportunities for the next quarter.

A – Avoid losses. When learning is not clearly linked to business goals, team members may want to avoid spending time on learning as they need to spend time on work aligned to the results that they are responsible for. Through showing how learning will support the achievement of business goals and discussing it as a team, it will help the team members see that the benefit of the learning can be worth the time spent on it.

T – Towards the default. In follow-up to the QBR, another option is to send a calendar invite for a regular weekly time for learning for the team. Even if team members need to move the timeslot to fit their own calendar, they will see a clear expectation of how much time to spend weekly in learning. And by having a shared recurring calendar invite, even though team members would be doing their own individual learning during that time, it will provide a space for learning that can be discussed and can be used for collaboration in learning as needed. The recurring shared calendar invite becomes a default setting for learning for the team.

I – Incentives. Randomized rewards are very effective for incentive. Consider using randomized rewards for learning during the quarter for your team. By sharing spot prizes to recognize learning accomplishments, it will help team members commit time for learning and persevere in the face of setbacks.

C – Commitment. We like to stay consistent with our commitments. This can be built into the QBR and follow-up habit by having each team member share their learning plans as part of the QBRs. People are more likely to follow through on commitments if they have publicly committed to doing so.

YOUR ACTION PLAN

Whether you are already doing QBRs and linking learning to the discussion, or if you have yet to establish a cadence of QBRs, here are some considerations to build your own action plan to move forward:

- Do you have a regular schedule of QBRs? If not, can you establish one?
- Would your QBR be in person or virtual? How would you manage the meeting based on this? Would you need to plan for both in person attendees and virtual ones?

- How much time would you block for a QBR?

- Do you already have an established agenda and would you need to change it to include reflection, learning and follow-up?

- What type of icebreaker or fun activity would work for your team?

- Do you need to adjust the agenda to ensure that every voice is equally heard? And how can you ensure that less vocal team members share their reflection and learning?

- Does your team have clear key performance indicators and do you already know what learning materials align to the results needed? If not, see Chapter 6 AIM to LEARN.

- What blockers or obstacles should you consider in looking to use this habit with your team? How will you work around them?

- What would the follow-up message look like for your team? Would you use a calendar invite for learning for the team?

- Based on the habit as described in this chapter, draw your own version of the cue, routine, reward and context so that you have your own customized habit to move forward and implement.

- What is your first step to get started in using this habit?

Back to our story

What was missing from that team's QBRs that we discussed at the beginning of the chapter? The QBRs were designed well to discuss each person's positives, negatives and opportunities, but learning wasn't explicitly on the agenda. People would informally mention sharing some materials but that was ad hoc and there was no follow-up. There was no mechanism to ensure that learning was included and followed up. By changing the agenda and routine to include sharing learning suggestions as part of the standard agenda and sending a follow-up after the meeting, this can be the mechanism to ensure the team is well set up to accomplish their key performance indicators.

Returning to Amazon, what mechanism do they use to make their QBRs more effective? Amazon is a writing culture, so they use a written report in preparation for business reviews (as well as many other meetings). The report needs to be written succinctly and is shared with leadership for feedback. The author of the report can learn from the reflection built into the writing and the feedback received. It is part of the Amazon culture to write, reflect and learn in this way, and the written report is the mechanism they use to ensure this happens as part of the QBR (Carney, 2021).

What mechanism are you using to ensure your team gets the most out of the QBR? And if you aren't currently doing QBRs, perhaps this is a mechanism you could start to employ.

Key takeaways

- A QBR can be an effective reflection and learning point for a team. By building learning into the QBR and follow-up, it links learning to business results in a concrete way.

TABLE 11.1 Make the quarterly business reviews and follow-ups habit AUTOMATIC

AUTOMATIC	Quarterly business reviews and follow ups habit ...
Allow for feeling good To get it done, make it fun.	During the QBR, include an icebreaker or activity that is fun and engaging for the team.
Under the influence If the leader is a gem, we'll follow them.	After the QBR and follow-up message, as a manager, mention in a team meeting how you are doing with your own learning to share your own example.
Tip the scale If we can't see it, we often won't do it.	Have team members share in team meetings how they are continuing to learn, or what recommendations for learning they would share with the team.
Ownership If it's mine, I think it's super fine.	Name a theme for the learning during the quarter and refer to the learning with the theme for the team; to foster a sense of ownership for the team.

(continued)

TABLE 11.1 (Continued)

AUTOMATIC	Quarterly business reviews and follow ups habit …
Mindset As a skill set grows, our fixed mindset will decompose.	Reflecting on the previous quarter and discussing learning plans will foster a growth mindset across the team.
Avoid losses Don't ignore a potential gain just because a loss would be a pain.	By setting the expectation that learning aligns to key performance indicators, and reinforcing this, you are letting employees know they are not losing by spending time on learning.
Towards the default To be quick, go with the default pick.	Consider making the follow-up note a calendar timeslot instead – so everyone has the time on their calendars by default.
Incentives A bird in the hand is worth two in the bush.	Consider giving spot incentives to those who are achieving their learning goals.
Commitment If I say it, I better do it.	As part of the learning discussion during the QBR, consider having each team member share what they will commit to doing for learning over the next quarter.

References

Amazon Web Services (2022) *AWS Well Architected Framework* [online] https://docs.aws.amazon.com/wellarchitected/latest/operational-readiness-reviews/building-mechanisms.html [Accessed 24 September 2022]

Carney, M (2021) *Value(s): Building a better world for all*, Signal, McClelland and Stewart, Toronto

12

Team meetings

Team meetings can be an effective place to include learning. Managers are the key component to set the tone and make this work or not work. In speaking with Scott Matthews, a learning and development professional with over 20 years' experience in the insurance industry, he shared a relevant story about the effectiveness of team meetings and the manager's influence (Matthews, 2022). There was a technology team, and the manager set the tone for the group. This particular manager set a minimum amount of time that everyone was expected to learn during their work week. The timing was flexible for the group so that they could fit it into their work in a way that worked for them.

Being a technology team in an agile environment meant that the team's work was planned in two-week sprints. Agile is a way of working that enables a team to release material every two weeks and adjust their work based on their findings as they go along, rather than gathering all the requirements up front and then working on a product for months at a time for one large release.

Many companies are moving to agile ways of working, even outside of technology teams. In today's challenging and ever-changing environment, agile is becoming more and more prevalent as companies look to work in a nimble and flexible manner. Given this type of work environment, how did this team in particular ensure that learning was prioritized?

We'll find that out a little later, but let's have a look at our habit for this chapter first – team meetings.

Overview of the habit

The learning habit for team meetings is quite simple – you include learning on the agenda. It doesn't have to take long but it needs to be done regularly. By doing so, you show social proof of learning and you make it an expected behaviour to learn, share learning and to find opportunities to apply learning. The team benefits from this collaboration and the learning done by individuals, it is then compounded by sharing with the group and encouraging others to learn. It can seem simple but team meetings are regular meetings and including learning is one of the most effective and habit-forming ways to encourage learning within a team.

Michelle Tong, a Global Director of Learning and Development with an international telecommunications firm, has worked in learning and development for over ten years, primarily with tele-communications and insurance companies (Tong, 2022). Michelle shared how she has seen effective use of a 'meeting-in-a-box' to make it easy for managers to include learning in their team meet-ings. A meeting-in-a-box is a quick kit, usually in the form of slides with speaker notes, that gives a manager a 5–10 minute section for their team meeting with resources to use to discuss learning. Steve Turner, head of learning for a major multinational manufacturing firm (Turner, 2022), has seen this be used effectively as well – includ-ing for topics like diversity, equity and inclusion.

> Team meetings are a powerful forum to change the social norms and by including learning, it can help set the stage for learning and collaboration across a team.

Another manager story comes from a manager who was curious about how to have an effective team meeting. This individual had been a people leader for a number of years, but in a new role with a new company, he wanted to ensure he was doing the best he could to set up his team for success. He recognized that the team meeting was a key component that he could leverage to enable his team to share and collaborate and learn together, but he wasn't sure how to optimize his meetings. So he observed a few team meetings from successful managers in the company and then integrated what they were doing into his own meetings. They had standard agendas that included learning. This manager realized the agenda was the mechanism he could use to build the best team meeting. He set up an agenda and used it every week with his team, and it included learning. It was flexible to meet the demands of the business and the time of the quarter, but it included standard items that provided a structure within which the team could work and learn. And a bonus was that if the manager was away or unable to attend, the agenda was already set and could be run by one of the team members. In this way, this manager optimized the time and energy his team spent in their meeting together, and he built learning into the flow of what they were doing every week.

An important lesson learned with this habit is that it needs to be led by the manager and not forced on the group. When a manager requires everyone to share a learning or reflection in every meeting it can become a burden for the group instead of an insightful and collaborative process. Further, if the manager themselves does not share learning or areas they are looking to improve, but expects the team to do this, it sets the wrong tone and turns people off. Carol Harper knows this all too well after 30 years working in learning and development at a major financial institution. As Carol shares, a manager who forces the team to share, instead of setting themselves as the example and leaving it open to the team to share, can destroy the positive intent of the initiative. Instead, she recommends the manager leads by example, and people can choose to follow. When the manager provides a strong example and asks but does not require others to share, it makes this habit much more effective (Harper, 2022).

Cue

The cue for this habit is the team meeting itself. If you don't already have a regular team meeting on the calendar, then as you consider using this habit, it's a good time to send an invite for a recurring meeting. During COVID, and continuing as organizations work in hybrid environments, it is a good idea to have a team meeting on the calendar as a space for regular updates and collaboration. Whereas office environments before COVID may have been less structured in their team collaboration as people were face to face in the office, now with remote and hybrid working, it is good to have a meeting invite on the calendar and include a virtual link for those who are working remotely that day.

Routine

Where this learning habit may be different from what you are doing now in your team meeting, is that the routine includes **learning on the agenda**. Add it to your standard agenda (or create a standard agenda) where the team has time set aside to discuss relevant learning, either recent learning or planned learning. If you have followed the QBR and follow-up habit, then this is a great time to check in on how learning is going based on what was discussed in the QBR. With the team altogether in the meeting, it is also a good time to celebrate any recent wins or provide recognition for learning. This can be quite informal but leave space on the agenda to randomly recognize people as they progress in their learning journey.

Reward

With this habit, the reward is **the team supports each other's development**. There is **recognition for learning**, which is a reward for the team members. Through the inclusion of learning and subsequent discussion the team can **uncover new opportunities and innovation**. The rewards build up over time as well, so when this habit becomes the norm, the team will see incremental improvement (Clear, 2018).

As with other positive habits, the more it is done, the greater the gains over time.

FIGURE 12.1 Team meetings habit

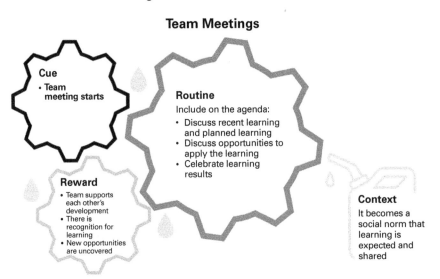

Context

The context with this habit is that it changes the social norm on the team. This can build up over time. It becomes the norm that learning is expected and shared. This may seem like a small thing but is a powerful social norm to enable on a team. With teams where learning is expected and shared, people innovate and collaborate more, teams can become more engaged and it can attract others to join the team.

Measurement for the habit

To measure this habit you can look to how often team meetings are happening, how often they include learning and then you can also consider related measures like evidence of learning and learning impact, which this habit influences and supports.

From the list of measurements below, consider which ones you have access to measure, and which ones you could add to measure. As always, you'll want to balance the need to measure with the ease of compiling the measurement, as measurement is a check on the impact of adding learning to team meetings, but the measurement is not the main goal. Measurement provides one feedback mechanism to see if the habit is working as intended. In addition, you can use the measurement to determine what good looks like for your team. Decide on your target for the measurement and then track against that target.

- Team meeting frequency – how often do you meet?
- Team meeting with learning – how often does the team discuss learning in the meeting?
- Team meeting discussion – how many people on the team share learning?
- Team meeting discussion – often does the manager share learning in the meeting?
- Team meeting recognition – how often is learning recognized in the meeting?
- Innovation on the team – what examples of innovation have surfaced as a result of learning discussions?
- Team engagement – what are the results for the team on employee engagement surveys and any questions related to learning and development?
- Team attrition – what is the evidence of whether people want to stay on the team or join the team?

Additional related measures:

- If your company has individual learning plans in a system, how many team members are filling them in? How often is the learning indicated completed? How often are the plans updated?
- If your company has online learning, is there evidence of learning usage available for your team that relates to the discussion in your team meetings?
- How is your team performing on their key performance indicators, before and after including learning in team meetings?
- Is there a similar team that is not discussing learning in team meetings, and how do measurements like attrition, engagement, and innovation compare to that team?

Make this habit AUTOMATIC

A – Allow for feeling good. To make the adoption of this habit easier, make it fun and light. We know that if sharing learning is forced, it will backfire, so look to make it engaging and enjoyable. If your organization has resources for team meetings, like the meeting-in-a-box, look to use these materials and keep it fun. If you are responsible for organizational learning, consider creating a meeting-in-a-box to make it easy for managers to include learning in their team meetings.

U – Under the Influence. The manager sets the tone for the team meeting so be aware of this. If you are the manager, share your own learning and ask your team (but do not require them) to share their learning as well. If you are responsible for organizational learning and looking to enable teams to adopt this habit, share examples of how managers can effectively influence their teams. Look to have an influential executive share how they include learning in their team meetings with direct reports.

T – Tip the scale. Success can be shared, and it will help others to get on board. If there's a manager in your organization who is using this habit effectively, consider having them share their story. Or if you are a manager yourself, seek out managers who are using this habit and find out how they have made it work for their team. These success stories can be shared in communication channels to encourage others to adopt this habit.

O – Ownership. To increase the sense of ownership of this habit, name the item on the agenda that shares learning. If you are responsible for corporate learning, you could include a sample agenda in materials you share with managers, and encourage them to customize the agenda and materials to make it their own.

M – Mindset. In sharing learning in meetings, you'll want to ensure a growth mindset is encouraged. If you are a manager, look for resources that your organization shares, or materials available publicly, about how to provide growth mindset feedback. If you are responsible for organizational learning, consider sharing a tip sheet for managers on how to provide growth mindset feedback.

A – Avoid losses. Help everyone get onboard with this habit by sharing recognition in a positive way and creating a safe space to share learning in team meetings. If you are a manager, ensure you don't penalize anyone for not sharing their learning in a meeting, instead encourage the behaviour that you'd like to see and model it yourself.

T – Towards the default. With this habit, it shouldn't be unusual to share learning experiences in a team meeting. If you are responsible for organizational learning, consider sharing a standard agenda for team meetings that includes learning and include it in onboarding materials. Reinforce this concept during company-wide meetings and ongoing communications.

I – Incentives. Is there a way you can provide incentives to those demonstrating the use of this habit? If you are a manager, consider incentives to recognize learning accomplishments. If you manage learning for the organization, consider incentives or recognition for managers who use this habit.

C – Commitment. To make this habit effective, managers need to commit to their own learning before they can expect their team to get on board. If you are a manager, consider how you have committed. If you manage learning for the organization, consider how you help managers commit to their own learning.

YOUR ACTION PLAN

As you consider your team meeting and look to include learning, to follow this habit, consider these questions to formulate your action plan:

- Do you already have a team meeting cadence set up? How frequent is it?
- Do you have a good set-up for both remote and onsite participants?
- Do you have an established agenda and how is it shared?
- Do you already include learning informally and occasionally in your team meeting?
- How would you build and share an agenda that standardizes including learning and reflection?
- How would you ensure that including learning and reflection is not a forced exercise?

- Are there team members you can speak to, to get their help in enabling the team to adopt this habit?
- Do you have a way to track some of the measurements mentioned? Which ones? What are your targets?
- Write down how you will get started with this habit and give yourself a timeline to begin.

Back to our story

So how did that technology team manage to ensure learning happened on their team? Their manager built it into the structure of how the team did their work. In their team meetings, discussing learning was included right along with work updates. It was a standard part of the agenda. But even more than that, the manager used their work tracking system, an industry standard ticketing system, to track their work including learning. The ticketing system uses tickets to track work as it moves through the process from idea or issue to full release. Learning items were not just talked about in the team meetings; the team would include tickets for learning items to ensure the work was prioritized and tracked. In this way, learning was truly part of their flow of work. Team members were expected to complete work indicated in the ticketing system, and learning was listed and expected right there in the system along with their other work. This manager had huge success both on the team's metrics and in evidence of learning for his team. Much like we discussed in the previous chapter, as Amazon does, this team had created a mechanism to ensure that work included the necessary learning.

Key takeaways

- Team meetings are one of the most effective vehicles to foster learning at the team level

- By including learning as a component of every team meeting, companies can ensure that work includes the learning needed for the team

TABLE 12.1 Make the team meetings habit AUTOMATIC

AUTOMATIC	Team meetings habit ...
Allow for feeling good To get it done, make it fun.	Provide fun talking tips for team meetings.
Under the influence If the leader is a gem, we'll follow them.	Have a popular executive share how they include learning in their team meetings.
Tip the scale If we can't see it, we often won't do it.	Share results of team meetings/collaboration on learning in communications.
Ownership If it's mine, I think it's super fine.	Provide managers with sample agendas for team meetings and encourage them to customize them for their groups while including learning.
Mindset As a skill set grows, our fixed mindset will decompose.	Share tips for growth mindset feedback for managers.
Avoid losses Don't ignore a potential gain just because a loss would be a pain.	Share how learning can help innovation and development – and share recognition.
Towards the default To be quick, go with the default pick.	Share a standard team meeting agenda that includes learning by default.
Incentives A bird in the hand is worth two in the bush.	Give random prizes to managers or employees using this habit.
Commitment If I say it, I better do it.	Have managers commit to including learning in their own development plans.

References

Clear, J (2018) *Atomic Habits: An easy and proven way to build good habits & break bad ones*, Avery, New York

Harper, C (2022) Director, Leadership, Learning and Development (retired) [Interview] (29 April 2022)

Matthews, S (2022) Director, Technology and Analytics Learning [Interview] (21 April 2022)

Tong, M (2022) Global Director of Learning and Development [Interview] (2 May 2022)

Turner, S (2022) Global Head of Learning and Skills [Interview] (14 April 2022)

13

Manager one-on-one

In March 2020, when COVID restrictions came into place, routines and habits were changed on a rapid and far-reaching scale. For those who shifted from working in an office to working remotely, managers could no longer drop by someone's desk and ask how things were going. Chance chats in the hallway were no longer available to check in with employees. For managers who wanted to ensure they maintained regular one-on-one contact with each team member, they needed to book regular recurring one-on-ones with each member of their teams.

During this time, one manager of a technology team decided to help her team and provide space for learning. She encouraged her team to spend part of every Friday afternoon on learning, and she checked in with each team member during their one-on-one meeting to discuss the development time and how it was going.

The manager would use the dashboards available to her from the company learning systems to reference what areas employees were learning and how they were progressing with their learning. She would also ask about other areas, outside the learning systems, that the employees were using for their development and what they were finding useful.

The manager took ideas from these one-on-one discussions to cross-pollinate ideas for development on her team. She would suggest team members connect if she found they were learning about the same areas. She would also encourage team members to reach out to others on the team who had mastered areas that the team member was interested in.

How did her team feel about this new habit? First let's look at the manager one-on-one habit, and we can come back to our story.

Overview of the habit

This habit takes the manager one-on-one and adds development to the discussion. A manager one-on-one is a regular meeting between one direct report and their manager. Typically, the meeting is 30 minutes to an hour in length and occurs weekly or bi-weekly. Generally, when the meeting is established the manager and employee agree on the parameters of the meeting – what topics will be regularly included, what metrics will be discussed (if any) and then meetings generally follow that established routine. For consistent one-on-ones, a regular recurring invite is established so that the meeting is on both people's calendars.

> Manager one-on-ones are an important connection, especially in hybrid/remote working environments.

Michelle Tong, a global learning and development director, recommends making learning a part of the discussion in regular one-on-ones. If it's just done during an annual performance review, people forget what they talked about. Instead, Michelle recommends the manager sets the tone, includes learning and keeps it organic to support the employee (Tong, 2022).

Cue

The cue for this habit is the scheduled manager one-on-one meeting. Ideally, this is a recurring calendar invite on both people's calendars that is only shifted occasionally. If managers shift the timeslot or repeatedly cancel their one-on-ones, their team may perceive this as the manager not prioritizing the team and it can be a factor in employee disengagement. It can also lead to less productivity and efficiency as employees reach out with non-urgent questions more often as they don't know when they will have time with their manager (Saunders, 2015).

Routine

The routine for this habit is to **have an established flexible agenda that includes discussing development**. The development component of the discussion can be as simple as the manager asking if the employee has found any useful resources or learning material that is helping them in their role or checking in on how learning discussed earlier is going. The employee can share development opportunities they would like to participate in – such as stretch assignments, upcoming event-based learning or accessing additional learning material with the support of the company. The manager can share what they themselves have found useful in the past, and methods that they used to learn new ways of doing things. Through the discussion, the pair can identify opportunities to apply recent learning, which will help build skills and adapt the learning to how work is done on the team. This may also lead to new opportunities for the employee, within the team and potentially in new roles within the company.

If the team is using the quarterly business review and follow-up habit, then the manager one-on-one is a great time to touch base on the learning aligned to the initiatives and key results for the quarter. The manager can ask how the learning is going, and share what is working well for others on the team, as appropriate. The employee can give feedback on the learning and how it is going for their work. Together the manager and employee can adjust the expectations if needed, with a view to supporting the results with the best development options possible.

The manager one-on-one is also a great time to touch base on recent company-wide meetings, and if learning was discussed in those company-wide meetings, to discuss the employee's thoughts on the effectiveness and key insights from the meeting. Similarly, if the company is using the fiscal year start habit, the manager can support the expectations laid out, in an informal but very influential way, by checking in on learning that was shared at the start of the fiscal year.

With companies that are using executive-led dedicated time for learning, the manager one-on-one is a great place to check in and see how the learning is progressing. By discussing the executive-led dedicated time in the manager one-on-one, the manager shows that they support the learning time and they follow up on the expectation that the time is being used for learning and that the employee is benefiting from the protected time. The manager is a key component in helping employees feel supported in using the dedicated time and ensuring it is meeting the needs of both the employee and the company's expectations. By including this check-in about the dedicated time in the manager one-on-one, the manager is keeping the learning salient and reinforcing the expectations set by the company. Also if accessible and relevant, the manager can use dashboards with learning data for the team and team member to support the discussion and provide talking points.

THE USE OF DATA SHOULD BE DONE WITH A FOCUS ON LEARNING, NOT ON INSPECTION

If the manager uses the data regularly to berate or chastise employees for not completing mandatory learning, this weaponizes the data and is not supportive of a growth mindset for the team member. Instead, if the manager uses any supporting dashboards as one input to the discussion and references the data in an open and curious way to chat with the employee, the data can support the conversation in a positive manner and lead to further insight for both manager and employee.

For effective one-on-ones, the discussion can be flexible to meet the needs of both the manager and the employee for that particular week. By including learning as a standard item, the manager and employee can get into a cadence of regularly discussing learning and insights, and this can provide opportunities for innovation and learning on both sides.

Reward

The reward for this habit is that **the employee feels supported in their development.** As evidenced in the routine section above, the manager one-on-one provides a forum where the manager can show support for the other learning habits within the organization, such as fiscal year start, dedicated time for learning, quarterly business reviews and follow-up. As learning is discussed and new insights surface, opportunities for innovation and application can be brought to light, benefiting both the employee and the team. The discussion can also serve as a reward in itself, as the employee can get manager recognition for learning, and surface new opportunities.

Context

By including learning in every manager one-on-one; it supports the social norm of learning on the team. The context for this habit is that it **becomes an expectation that learning is regularly occurring and shared.** The team builds a social norm that the manager is supportive of learning and that team members regularly discuss and get feedback on their learning.

FIGURE 13.1 Manager one-on-one habit

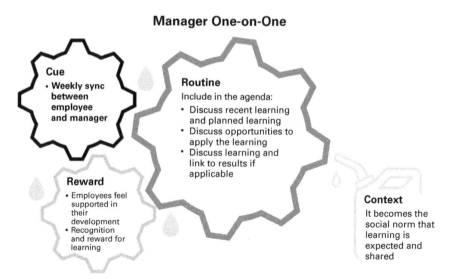

Manager One-on-One

Cue
• Weekly sync between employee and manager

Routine
Include in the agenda:
• Discuss recent learning and planned learning
• Discuss opportunities to apply the learning
• Discuss learning and link to results if applicable

Reward
• Employees feel supported in their development
• Recognition and reward for learning

Context
It becomes the social norm that learning is expected and shared

Measurement for the habit

To measure this habit, you can monitor how often one-on-ones are happening and whether the content of those one-on-one's includes development discussion. You can also look at evidence of the effectiveness of this habit by monitoring learning results, impact on key performance indicators and other evidence of effectiveness or opportunity. You can consider setting a target for both the usage of the habit and the evidence of its effectiveness. The measurement can provide one component of the feedback you use to tweak the habit continually to be as effective as possible.

If you are responsible for corporate learning and want to measure this habit across groups, you could also consider comparing the results of a team using the habit and a similar team that is not using the habit. In this way, you have a control group (the team not using the habit) to contrast the results of the use of the habit from the team participating. If other factors are similar, a difference in results between the two teams could be an indication that the habit is making the difference. Here are some metrics to consider:

- manager one-on-one frequency
- manager one-on-one agenda – including learning
- team metrics such as learning plans included in human resource management system
- employee surveys results, such as engagement surveys asking about development opportunities
- metrics of learning use from corporate systems such as a learning experience platform or learning management system; or learning dashboards available
- for corporate-wide measurement, number of managers viewing learning dashboard analytics

Make this habit AUTOMATIC

A – Allow for feeling good. The learning discussion in the manager one-on-one can be a positive and engaging discussion. Support managers in how to discuss learning with a positive, growth mindset focus. If you are a manager yourself, find resources online about how to give growth mindset feedback and ensure that the tone you set in the meeting is development-focused and not punitive. If you are using data in the discussion, use it to highlight accomplishments rather than to inspect the employee. The employee will be sensitive to any data that lends itself to a perception of big brother watching, so be sure to use that data to support the discussion, not to interrogate the employee.

U – **Under the influence.** Your leadership team can provide influential examples of how to integrate learning into one-on-one meetings. If you're responsible for corporate learning, consider asking an executive to share how they integrate learning into their one-on-ones. They could share this in a leadership meeting, or in a short message to their direct reports in support of effective one-on-ones. The more people in the organization hear that others are using the manager one-on-one habit and how they are doing it, the more likely others will start (Dolan et al, 2010).

T – **Tip the scale.** Managers can support each other in this habit. Consider establishing a collaboration channel for effective one-on-ones or using an existing channel to discuss tips for effective one-on-ones. Some companies look to have short challenges with ideas weekly for effective one-on-ones, to give managers ideas about what to do and keep effective coaching and discussion tips readily available.

O – **Ownership.** Individual employees who own their own development, embracing self-directed learning and a sense of personal mastery (Senge, 2006), will find the manager one-on-one habit supports their development. Adults who see learning as something forced upon them are less likely to engage in learning, and when they do engage in learning, they retain less of the material. For those employees, the manager one-on-one will feel like an inspection. Managers can be sensitive to the level of personal mastery in their employees and look to support them in moving towards personal mastery. Companies can encourage employees to own their own development and see their manager as a coach.

M – Mindset. To make this habit effective, managers need to act as a coach and mentor. If your company has materials to support managers as coaches, review those materials as a manager. If your company does not yet have coaching materials, use this as an opportunity to seek out resources for your own learning to build your coaching habit with a growth mindset focus.

A – Avoid losses. If you are responsible for corporate learning, you can support the adoption of this habit by making it easy for managers to use the habit. Share quick tips for manager one-on-ones, explain how to get to data for learning dashboards, help managers with coaching tips – and for all of these explain how the use of this habit will help managers to support their teams in reaching the results they need. Managers may at first perceive this habit as adding an item to their already busy one-on-ones, but by making it easy and linking the habit to business results, managers can begin to see how the adoption of this habit will make their jobs easier.

T – Towards the default. Make this habit the default for one-on-ones. If you're a manager, include notes or a link in the meeting invite to share the standard agenda, with learning included. If you have a number of managers reporting to you, share a standard agenda for one-on-ones to let them know about the expectation. And if you're responsible for learning in the organization, include a standard agenda for manager one-on-ones in onboarding and coaching materials.

I – Incentives. Incentives can be a powerful motivator, especially to get started with a new habit. If you are a manager and starting this habit yourself, decide on something that will motivate you to keep with this habit and then give yourself that reward when you hit your targets. If you are responsible for a group of managers, or for corporate learning, look to share incentives in a broader way. For example, one company that was looking to change manager coaching behaviour had a challenge per week, posted in their collaboration tool, with a points system to incentivize managers to get started and adopt the new coaching behaviour. The challenges had things like – 'Discuss learning in your one-on-one meetings this week and share your key insight here for a chance at a prize'. This provided incentives and it also shared the expectations across the management group.

C – Commitment. We know that we are more likely to follow through if we have publicly committed to a course of action. We are even more likely to achieve a goal if we have a partner to check in with regularly and hold us accountable (Kander, 2022). If you are a manager, pair up with someone to hold yourself accountable on your commitments for manager one-on-ones. For individual employees, the manager one-on-one can act as an accountability partner for learning, increasing employees' chances of achieving their goals to 95 per cent (Kander, 2022). If you are managing learning for your organization, look to encourage accountability partners to help your organization be successful with this habit.

YOUR ACTION PLAN

As you look to build this habit, consider your current state and where you'd like to adjust your current state:

- Do you already have an established cadence of one-on-ones?

    o If so, do you have a standard agenda?

    o Does the agenda include discussing development?

- If you don't yet have an established cadence of one-on-ones, how would you begin this?

- What will you include on the agenda?

- Do you have access to learning dashboards, for your own learning, or for your team's learning? If so, are you using them? If not, how will you start using them?

- Priorities change and focus can shift – how will you structure your one-on-ones to be flexible to cover topics as needed?

- Does your team have development materials identified? Does the team know what development materials will support their key performance indicators? If not, consider coming together as a group to discuss what development materials will support the team's needs, potentially using the quarterly business review and follow-up habit from Chapter 11.

- What action can you do today to establish regular one-on-ones and how will you integrate development discussions?

Back to our story

What was the result of the manager who encouraged her team to learn every Friday afternoon and checked in about how it was going in each one-on-one? Her team appreciated the support and encouragement, and it showed. They used the learning time productively, and compared to similar teams whose managers didn't use the one-on-ones the same way, this team had increased engagement in learning as measured by assessments and courses used. On quarterly employee engagement surveys, her team reported feeling supported in their development and showed overall increased engagement scores. They indicated they felt supported in their career development, they felt they could see themselves growing their career with the company, and they indicated they would recommend the company to a friend as a great place to work.

Even more telling, during the Great Resignation when many people shifted jobs or left the workforce in the latter phases of the COVID pandemic, her team did not have any resignations and had significantly lower attrition. The only team members who left the team were those promoted internally to alternative roles within the company. In comparison, similar teams who did not discuss development during one-on-ones or use the learning dashboards for discussion, suffered from increased attrition and saw people resign their positions from the company altogether.

When restrictions eased in 2022, and her team shifted to a hybrid model of partial remote and partial in office working, her team continued this habit. They kept their one-on-ones, meeting either in person or virtually depending on people's schedules, and maintained the same agenda including development. This story, based on several real life examples, illustrates how a manager took a massive shift in the way people work, caused by the COVID pandemic, and turned it into a positive by establishing a strong connection with her team members and providing them space to discuss their development.

Key takeaways

- Manager one-on-ones that include learning in the agenda are a key habit to support individuals' development.
- Manager one-on-ones that include learning will also support other learning habits in the organization, such as fiscal year start, executive-led dedicated time for learning, company-wide meetings, and quarterly business reviews and follow-up.

TABLE 13.1 Make the manager one-on-one habit AUTOMATIC

AUTOMATIC	Manager one-on-one habit ...
Allow for feeling good To get it done, make it fun.	Managers can make the learning discussion positive and upbeat.
Under the influence If the leader is a gem, we'll follow them.	Have a popular executive share how they include learning in their one-on-ones.
Tip the scale If we can't see it, we often won't do it.	Have a collaboration channel for managers to share stories of how their one-on-ones are going.
Ownership If it's mine, I think it's super fine.	Encourage employees to own their development and to see their managers as their coach – not the person who will tell them what to do with learning.
Mindset As a skill set grows, our fixed mindset will decompose.	Encourage managers to get comfortable in the role of learning coach.
Avoid losses Don't ignore a potential gain just because a loss would be a pain.	Make it easy for managers to include development in one-on-ones – give them talking points, data dashboards, etc.
Towards the default To be quick, go with the default pick.	Make a standard format for one-on-ones and share with managers.

(continued)

TABLE 13.1 (Continued)

AUTOMATIC	Manager one-on-one habit ...
Incentives A bird in the hand is worth two in the bush.	Give random recognition to managers who are having regular one-on-ones and speaking about learning.
Commitment If I say it, I better do it.	Look for opportunities to share a public commitment to coaching in one-on-ones.

References

Dolan, P, Hallsworth, M, Halpern, D, King, D and Vlaev, I (2010) Mindspace: Influencing behavior through public policy (report online)

Kander, D (2022) 3 strategies for holding yourself accountable, *Harvard Business Review* [online] https://hbr.org/2022/02/3-strategies-for-holding-yourself-accountable (archived at https://perma.cc/99A8-XH4V)

Saunders, E G (2015) Cancelling one-on-one meetings destroys your productivity, *Harvard Business Review* [online] https://hbr.org/2015/03/cancelling-one-on-one-meetings-destroys-your-productivity (archived at https://perma.cc/X4MY-378L)

Senge, P (2006) *The Fifth Discipline: The art and practice of the learning organization*, Currency Doubleday, New York

Tong, M (2022) Global Director of Learning and Development [Interview] (2 May 2022)

14

Performance review follow-ups

Across the 200+ companies that I've worked with over the last 25 years, helping them design and use learning programmes extended by the reach of technology, there has been a common theme. If companies can tie learning content to existing processes in the organization, more people will use the learning content. And one of the common existing processes is the performance review process.

A performance review is a discussion between the manager and employee about how the employee is doing in the job. Discussions about pay and promotions are sometimes included in the review, but they can also be done separately. Generally, the employee and the manager will individually fill in a form assessing the employee's performance against certain criteria specific to the job; often this is in the form of competencies needed for performing the role. The review is generally annual but can be done more often, depending on the company and the individual manager.

Many companies encourage managers to discuss learning and development (L&D) during performance reviews. Some companies have learning contracts or development plans that employees fill in at the beginning of the year, to commit to an action plan for their learning. Research shows us that if we discuss plans with someone else, and if we commit to plans in writing, we are much more likely to follow through on those plans (Kander, 2022).

The performance review is a powerful check point to discuss learning and make plans for the next year. But across the companies that

I've worked with, I've seen a trend that shows the process is not quite working as designed. And this trend indicates employees are missing out on many of the benefits of learning. What is that trend? We'll come back to that later, but let's look at our next habit now.

Overview of the habit

Many companies have established processes for annual performance reviews, including key components of the discussion and guidance on documentation and expectations. The performance review can be a useful reflection point to review highlights of the previous year and decide on goals for the next year. Some companies today also question the time and energy spent in performance reviews, and look to ensure that weekly or bi-weekly check-ins with regular coaching are part of the company culture instead (Buckingham and Goodall, 2015). If performance feedback only happens once a year, then that is cause for concern. The performance review format can also focus the discussion on items that have already happened, instead of providing a forum for looking forward to work that is happening now or will be happening shortly.

When performance reviews provide an annual reflection point in combination with regular coaching in one-on-ones, it can make for targeted feedback that can support high performance. To build expertise, we need targeted feedback and spaced practice to improve performance (Epstein, 2019) and the combination of annual reviews and regular coaching can help support that in the workplace. Spaced practice is when we learn something, leave it for a little while, and then come back to it later. This spaced practice helps to make learning more durable and better retained as it supports the process of moving new learning into our long-term memory (Epstein, 2019).

How does this tie into our habit? With learning goals included as part of the discussion in a performance review, then this habit is an add-on to that process and includes the manager sending a follow-up to book time to check in on the learning goals at regular intervals. This could be done as part of an established one-on-one meeting or it could be kept as a separate but ongoing meeting cadence. The important thing is to set the expectation that the learning goals will be revisited regularly to support ongoing learning, rather than being left to the next year's performance review.

This habit helps the manager support team members in their learning. It also helps the team member to make learning a regular part of their year, rather than something that they are scrambling to complete right before the next performance review.

Cue

The cue for this habit is the completion of the performance review where learning was discussed. Performance reviews are generally held near the end of the fiscal year or near the beginning of the new fiscal year. Often, there are systems in place to remind managers that they need to book time with employees to hold performance reviews. The process of promotions or compensation adjustments may be dependent on the completion of performance reviews, so there are a lot of dependencies (or additional cues) that support the completion of performance reviews. This helps to make this habit stick better, as it ties to an existing cue that is in itself tied to a number of existing cues in the organization.

Routine

The routine for this habit is to discuss learning in the review and send a follow-up after the performance review to discuss the learning plans progress and opportunities to apply the learning. This two-part follow-up discussion, on a regular and recurring basis, can be an informal discussion and it can be led by the employee, but it needs to be recurring and suggested by the manager.

KEEP L&D PRIORITIZED AND HELP THE EMPLOYEE FEEL SUPPORTED

In situations where the learning is discussed during the performance review and then not mentioned again, the employee may feel that they should spend their time in other areas and not follow up on the learning. They may have the impression that time spent in learning is seen as not work focused and is de-prioritized. The employee and the manager may both forget about the learning discussion and focus on getting the job at hand done. Without the benefit of learning, insight and innovation that may have happened if the time had been spent on development is lost. When the learning is part of a regular and recurring follow-up discussion, then both the manager and employee can remember what they discussed in the performance review and reflection, and continue with the learning by spending the time on the development and discussing how it's going periodically. This can help keep the commitment in mind for both the manager and the employee and ensure that the employee feels supported in their learning and understands the expectation for learning.

> The discussion about opportunities to apply the learning helps to make the learning stick – as it takes what may be industry knowledge and puts it in the context of how work is done in your organization.

This discussion can help both the manager and employee see how the learning can be used, what parts apply to their work context and what parts are not relevant. Through this discussion, opportunities and innovation surface, and the learning can be integrated into the ways of working and the mental frameworks that the employee brings to the job. Without a discussion about how to apply the learning, new tools, models and ideas are often left outside of the work, they are forgotten and not applied, and the learning is wasted.

> The manager is one of the most influential people on whether employees feel supported and encouraged to learn and innovate.

Through this follow-up discussion, the manager can show their support and demonstrate a commitment to supporting employee development. Through the discussion of opportunities to apply the learning, the learning can be integrated into how work is actually done, so that the time spent learning doesn't just help the employee but also helps the organization and the team.

Reward

The reward for this habit is that **the team is better supported to achieve key performance metrics.** The performance review provides an opportunity to discuss what's working well and what could be better; and align on learning that will support the employee in achieving their key performance indicators for the coming year. Through the habit outlined in this chapter, the employee and manager work together to support the continuous learning aligned to key performance indicators and regularly discuss together how the learning applies in the work context. This will help the employee to achieve the goals set out in the review discussion and help shift the learning from the abstract to actual application in the work context.

The team is also better supported in their development. While the majority of the learning may be aligned to key performance indicators and application on the job, this habit also supports development in general. And many employees report that a major reason they leave positions is that they do not feel supported in their development and they do not see any opportunities for development. By following this habit, the manager can support employees in their development goals and discuss opportunities to apply the new skills. This will help to support more engaged employees, which may show in **improved employee engagement scores and decreased turnover** (Vroman and Danko, 2022).

Context

The context for this habit is that learning is expected and shared. The team can shift from once-a-year performance reviews, to ongoing organic discussions that support the employees' development and help apply the learning on the job. As Michelle Tong (a global director of learning and development with an international telecommunications firm) shares, once the manager sets the expectation that learning will be a regular part of the discussion, then the discussion of learning can grow organically and become part of the way work is done, rather than a forced discussion (Tong, 2022).

FIGURE 14.1 Performance review follow-up habit

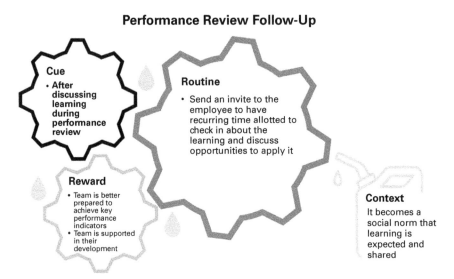

Performance Review Follow-Up

Cue
- After discussing learning during performance review

Routine
- Send an invite to the employee to have recurring time allotted to check in about the learning and discuss opportunities to apply it

Reward
- Team is better prepared to achieve key performance indicators
- Team is supported in their development

Context
It becomes a social norm that learning is expected and shared

> This habit should ideally support the employee to be a self-directed learner with a sense of personal mastery in their own development journey.

Measurement for the habit

To check your progress on this habit for your own use and across the organization, here are some potential measurement methods to see the use of the habit and the effectiveness of the habit:

- number of performance reviews completed
- number of learning plans completed
- number of performance reviews that include discussion of learning plans
- number of follow-ups sent after performance reviews – either through individual managers tracking for their own use or for organization-wide if the performance review system has this capability for tracking and reporting

- use of learning systems after performance reviews and per quarter following performance reviews
- employee engagement scores – particularly questions on development opportunities – for evidence of higher engagement/ indications of support for development, where this habit is in use
- comparison of employee engagement scores for teams where managers use this follow-up habit and where they do not use this follow-up habit
- comparison of performance metrics where managers use this follow-up habit and where they do not use this follow-up habit

As with other measurement suggestions, you'll want to determine what is feasible for measurement, preferably looking to items that are already being tracked and measured. You'll also want to have a mixture of measurement that shows the use of the habit and the effectiveness of the habit. The combination of these two areas will give you the feedback loop you need to get the most out of the habit and adjust it as needed to be more effective.

Make this habit AUTOMATIC

A – Allow for feeling good. With this habit, it would be easy to slip into making the follow-up discussions feel like a remediation plan or an inspection of the employee's learning progress. But that won't support learning and innovation and will make the follow-up feel like a chore. Instead keep the discussions focused on recognizing progress and supporting ongoing learning and generating ideas of how the learning applies and where it can be used. This habit should ideally support helping the employee be a self-directed learner with a sense of personal mastery in their own development journey. The manager is just there to provide context for learning at work as a coach, not as an inspector.

U – Under the influence. In support of this habit, look for opportunities for managers and executives to share their own learning, so that learning is more visible and recognized as ongoing. For example, some companies will host lunch and learns with a panel of leaders, to ask them about their learning and how they are applying it. When employees can hear and see that leaders are also learning; it helps make the social norm of learning regularly visible and supports their learning.

T – **Tip the scale.** A support to this habit can be to add discussing learning in team meetings. This will help cue learning for those on the team that didn't think they needed to focus on learning; as they will see others on the team are learning regularly. We are particularly influenced by those in the same groups as us, so hearing from other team members about how they have fit in learning to their jobs, will show those who are having trouble doing so that others in similar roles to them can do it (Cialdini, 2021).

O – **Ownership.** Sometimes employees expect to be told what to learn and look to the organization to provide a career path made for them. Organizations can provide opportunities and share resources, but employees need to decide on their own path and seek out opportunities that suit them. Employees need to own their own development, and the use of this habit should support that thinking. The manager can act as a supportive coach and help as an accountability partner on the learning the employee has committed to, but the habit overall should support the employee owning their own development.

M – **Mindset.** In the discussions on development, look to reassure employees that they are growing their current skill set, not that their current skill is deficient and needs fixing. Discussions can support growth rather than focusing on what is wrong and how to fix it. We learn best and continue with habits when we build on success and feel good, so the discussions need to be supportive and positive.

A – **Avoid losses.** Investing the time to follow up on learning can seem like a loss; it's important to remember how the learning ties to existing key performance indicators and supports achieving the results that the team needs. In this way, the learning becomes part of the work, rather than something that takes time away from the work that needs to be done.

T – Towards the default. Look for ways to make learning the default for the group. For example, follow-up messages can be shared in collaboration channels, to make them visible to the group and easy to share.

I – Incentives. If you're in a manager role and looking to use this habit, you could set yourself a reminder to send the notes out and then give yourself a small reward when you complete the task. Some people find marking an item as complete on a to-do list a reward for doing the item; others take a short five-minute refresh break after completing a task as a reward. Find a way to give yourself a short-term incentive for using the habit, to support the longer-term rewards identified in the habit overall.

C – Commitment. We know that having an accountability partner helps us achieve goals with more success, so using that strategy with this habit can work well too. Managers could pair up to hold each other accountable in using this habit. And employees can pair up to hold each accountable in their learning. For employees, this can be even more valuable as it provides them with a partner to discuss learning and ideas with, in addition to their manager. This form of paired commitment can support the use of this habit, and the ongoing learning.

YOUR ACTION PLAN

To put this habit into action, you could consider a few ways, depending on your role in the organization:

If you are responsible for the performance management system in the organization, you could consider adding a system check that would remind managers to send follow-ups after performance reviews. If you aren't using a formal performance management system, you could include guidance in your materials for managers to let them know to include a follow-up about learning.

If you are responsible for the learning systems in the organization, you could consider using the system to remind people to include follow-up discussions about their learning after performance reviews. There may be messaging capabilities in the learning system that can support this, or even calendar or goal setting features that can help.

If you are a manager and looking to use this habit with your own team, add a reminder to your calendar and block the time to send follow-ups to your team after your performance reviews. You could consider using your existing one-on-ones or team meetings as follow-ups to discuss learning and help support spaced practice on your team.

If you are an individual contributor, during your performance review discuss how you'll work with your manager to support discussions about learning and development. You could look to include it in your one-on-ones. And if part of your intended learning is event-based learning, you could ensure to include a follow-up with your manager or a share back point with your team to share what you've learned. This will help you understand and use the material better, and it will help your team and support collaboration.

How you use this habit will depend on your role and which other habits you already have in place. In any case though, you'll want to ensure you have a mechanism to support the cue and routine so that you'll see the benefits of using the habit.

Back to our story

What is the trend that I've seen across companies and for many years, when they discuss learning as part of performance reviews? The trend is a massive spike in learning by employees as the annual performance review approaches. People rush to complete what they committed to at the beginning of the year. Learning usage goes up by five times or more what is done in a regular month as everyone scrambles to get a completion before they meet with their manager. What does this show us? Learning is not being regularly discussed in manager one-on-ones and employees are leaving the learning to the last minute, and then rushing to complete it, having missed the opportunity to apply it during the year. They are simply checking the box on the completion, not using the learning to support their work during the year. And that is a missed opportunity. By integrating this habit, along with the manager one-on-one habit and others, the learning discussed during the performance review can actually be used to support performance, not just check the box and squeeze it in before the due date.

Key takeaways

- This habit ties to the performance review process within the organization; it adds a follow-up to include touchpoints about learning discussed in the review, to keep the learning ongoing and provide for feedback and spaced practice.

TABLE 14.1 Make the performance review follow-up habit AUTOMATIC

AUTOMATIC	Performance review follow-up habit ...
Allow for feeling good To get it done, make it fun.	Keep the focus on growth not remediation; keep messaging supportive.
Under the influence If the leader is a gem, we'll follow them.	Managers and executives can share what they are learning themselves to influence others to learn.
Tip the scale- If we can't see it, we often won't do it.	Discuss in team meetings how everyone is learning as a follow-up to reviews.
Ownership If it's mine, I think it's super fine.	Encourage employees to own their own development, with the manager as coach.
Mindset As a skill set grows, our fixed mindset will decompose.	Reassure employees that they are growing, not that their current skills are in question.
Avoid losses Don't ignore a potential gain just because a loss would be a pain.	As a manager, consider the benefits to having a team that is developing.

(continued)

TABLE 14.1 (Continued)

AUTOMATIC	Performance review follow-up habit ...
Towards the default To be quick, go with the default pick.	Use a collaboration channel to share follow-up with everyone.
Incentives A bird in the hand is worth two in the bush.	Put a reminder on your calendar to send the message out, then reward yourself when you mark it complete.
Commitment If I say it, I better do it.	Pair up with someone to hold yourself accountable.

References

Buckingham, M and Goodall, A (2015) Reinventing performance management, *Harvard Business Review* [online] https://hbr.org/2015/04/reinventing-performance-management (archived at https://perma.cc/4TUF-JT2W)

Cialdini, R B (2021) *Influence: The psychology of persuasion* - New and Expanded. New York: Harper Business

Epstein, D (2019) *Range: How generalists triumph in a specialized world*. Pan Macmillan, London

Kander, D (2022) 3 strategies for holding yourself accountable, *Harvard Business Review* [online] https://hbr.org/2022/02/3-strategies-for-holding-yourself-accountable (archived at https://perma.cc/N6NT-87N5)

Tong, M (2022) *Global Director of Learning and Development* [Interview] (2 May 2022)

Vroman, S R and Danko, T (2022) How to build a successful upskilling program, *Harvard Business Review* [online] https://hbr.org/2022/01/how-to-build-a-successful-upskilling-program (archived at https://perma.cc/3JLG-4UB2)

PART FOUR

Individual habits

15

Log-on learning

In 2020, when the pandemic shifted schools to virtual in many areas, habits changed for families with school-age children. There was one family, with two girls aged 10 and 12, where both parents already worked from home. Unlike many families with much larger changes to adjust to during the pandemic, this family just shifted their morning routine slightly. With the shift to virtual schooling, they no longer had to rush to make lunches in the morning and they didn't need to ensure the girls were ready and on the bus by 8.30 am. What does this illustrative story of a change in routine have to do with learning habits? We'll come back to that but first let's check out this habit.

Overview of the habit

Interweaving learning into your day is a powerful way to build continuous learning into how you work. Michelle Tong, global learning and development leader, shares how she encourages team members to interweave learning into how they are working (Tong, 2022). She encourages her team to build learning into what they do every day and says that by finding ways to build learning into how you work, you can learn and apply your new thinking immediately, building a virtuous cycle of learning into how you work. Michelle mentions that learning can take place anytime during the day in various forms, such as finding a crowd-sourced answer on sites like Quora or Reddit or reading a quick article while standing in line at the grocery store.

Learning can even take place subconsciously as often seen when acquiring language skills by immersing oneself into a culture or region.

But many people struggle with how to interweave learning into how they work. Steve Turner, head of global learning at a major multinational manufacturing firm, likes to think of interweaving learning into the 'cracks and crevices' of his day – and one trick he shared in particular is that if a meeting is cancelled at the last minute, he sees that as bonus time that he can use for learning, as he is now unexpectedly open (Turner, 2022). Using the cancelled meeting as a cue for learning is an example of using an existing cue to trigger learning. Another example of a cue is when you log on to your computer in the morning. That's where this habit – log-on learning – comes in.

When we start our day, for many people, it's a time that their circadian rhythms support deeper analytical thinking. According to Daniel Pink in his book *When: The Scientific Secrets of Perfect Timing*, the mornings are an ideal time for many people to do deeper work (Pink, 2018). This can support learning as we can use that analytical thinking to optimize taking in new information and think about ways to apply it as we look at the day ahead.

This habit uses the cue of logging on in the morning to start your day with some form of learning, such as reading, taking a course, doing an assessment, reviewing earlier notes on learning, or planning time to dive deeper into a subject. By tying learning to an existing daily morning cue, it makes learning a daily habit and brings the benefits of new insights, fresh thinking and innovation, into our individual daily way of working.

Cue

The cue for this habit is starting your computer in the morning. You can make this cue even stronger if you add a learning application or favourite resource to your start-up menu, so that the application where you want to access learning resources is available as one of the programmes that opens when you start up your computer. If you leave your computer on overnight and pick up where you left off, then you could add a routine of leaving the learning application or resource open the night before, so that it's the first thing you see when your computer comes out of sleep mode. If you don't work on a computer daily, you could modify this habit to use your phone as the trigger, and access a learning app there as you start your day.

Routine

The routine for this habit is to **spend some time with learning resources or reflecting on previous learning, as you start your day**. The routine can include reading an article, listening to a podcast, re-reading notes from previous learning, trying out some retrieval learning by doing an assessment or any other learning related activity that suits your goals. You could set a general timeframe for the learning and then vary this depending on your work that day. Setting an expectation of time will help so that whether you do more or less depending on the day, you can look to have an average across the week that supports your goals.

By doing this learning every day, you will space out your learning and have time to reflect and retrieve earlier learning, all of which will make your learning more durable and help you integrate what you learn into how you work.

Reward

The reward for this habit is that you will feel sharper and better prepared for your day, and in the longer term, as jobs shift and directions change, you will have spent time learning every day to help you better manage and adapt in the face of uncertainty. Rather than waiting until a job change forces learning, you will be in the habit of learning regularly, which will support you in identifying shifts and looking for opportunities that will support your goals. This habit will also provide you with new insights and ideas, making work more interesting, and helping you identify new opportunities in your work.

Context

The context for this habit is that learning is daily. By following this habit regularly, you make daily learning your default. It becomes part of how your day starts. And even though some days will allow for more learning times, and other days not allow any time, you will have the daily expectation of learning and it will start to weave itself into how you begin your day, and support how you work daily.

FIGURE 15.1 Log-on learning habit

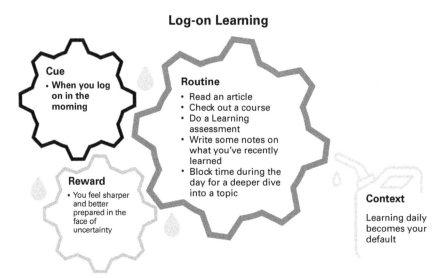

Measurement for the habit

To measure this habit in your own daily use, here are some suggested ways to track what you're doing and see if it's working for you:

- number of days where you included learning at the beginning of your day

- number of days in a row where you included learning at the beginning of your day (tracking a streak)

- average time spent learning daily
- ideas, projects, opportunities influenced by daily learning

To measure this habit at the organizational level, here are some suggested ways to see if it's happening in the organization and how effective it is:

- average time spent in learning by employees (note: this measure is limited to time spent in learning systems that can be reported on; consider having employees self-report this measure to capture learning done outside of learning systems)
- number of employees using learning systems daily
- percentage of employee population using learning systems daily
- percentage of employee population reporting increased opportunities or development (through survey sentiment)

Make it AUTOMATIC

A – Allow for feeling good. To make this a habit, start slowly and spend a few minutes daily learning. Also, begin with a topic that you are really curious about. In this way, you can make it easy to start and make it enjoyable. Then you can build on this success and follow your curiosity to other topics and ideas.

U – Under the influence. If you're looking to influence your organization to begin log-on learning, you could have influential leaders share how they learn daily. This can be shared in a newsletter, blog post or as a quick topic in a town hall meeting. By seeing how respected leaders use this habit, it will help others to try out this habit as well. You may have seen articles about the morning routines of successful people – titles such as 'The morning routines of highly successful people' or 'Top ten morning habits of successful people'. Try bringing a version to your organization with leaders that people know and respect.

T – Tip the scale. As with other continuous learning habits, it's not always visible that this habit is occurring. If you're looking to encourage your organization to follow this habit, consider doing a survey and capture stories from employees using this habit successfully, then share quotes or stories from the survey so others can see that this habit is possible.

O – Ownership. If you are building this habit into your own daily routine, think of the learning time as your own time, something that you are doing for yourself. Learning daily is a form of self-care and can help you build resilience and adaptability in the face of change. Daily learning time is your time.

M – Mindset. As you build learning into your daily routine, think of this learning as learning for growth. Just as with many of the other learning habits articulated in this book, the learning is for development, not for remediation. We do better when we feel good, and if you think of the learning as fixing your skill set rather than building your skill set, it will de-motivate you. Embrace a growth mindset for yourself.

A – Avoid losses. Start small with the learning time for this habit and build on your success. By starting small, you will avoid feeling a loss of time in your morning routine, as the learning time will be a small component of how you start your day. As you gain traction with the habit, you'll see benefits from the time you spend learning and the loss of time from your previous regular routine will fade in comparison to the benefit of daily learning.

T – Towards the default. Make it the default to start with learning by setting up your systems to support this. You could add a learning app to the home screen on your phone or add a learning application to the start-up on your computer. If you don't shut down your computer every evening, then open a tab or a programme for learning and leave it open for the morning so it's the first thing you see when you start at your computer. If you can reduce the friction to get started, you will support making it the default choice to begin with learning.

I – Incentives. There are many long-term incentives for learning daily such as increased resilience and adaptability over time. But you'll want to ensure you have some short-term incentives for each day. You could consider keeping a running total of your learning streak – the days in a row that you learn daily. Jerry Seinfeld does this to keep writing – he tracks each day he writes materials and maintains a streak. This keeps him on track as he doesn't want to break the streak and start again.

Many apps do this type of tracking for you as well so if the one you're using for learning has a tracking mechanism, you could use this to encourage your learning if you like that incentive. Find a short-term win that works for you and use that to encourage yourself.

C – Commitment. Look for ways to commit to daily learning and hold yourself accountable. You could include this commitment in your corporate learning plan or performance review. You could tell a peer that this is your plan, and if they are doing a similar plan, you could help each other achieve your goals.

YOUR ACTION PLAN

As you consider using this habit yourself, add a learning app to the start up on your computer to make it easy to begin learning when you log in. Think about if you will set up a way to learn on the weekends – perhaps with an app on your phone if you want to start your day with learning something outside of work on the weekends.

As you consider encouraging this habit in the organization, if you are in leadership or if you manage learning and development, think about the systems you currently have in place and if any can support log-on learning. Perhaps you can have an app added to the start-up menu on corporate computers, so that it is easy to access learning systems when people log on.

Whether you are going to use this habit yourself, or if you are enabling your organization to use it, consider:

- Do you have an existing cue for this habit? What is it? How could you make it better? How could you add one?

- Do you have a routine that is going to work for you? What routine would you recommend for others, if you're enabling this for the organization?

- Does the reward work? How could it work better? What type of reward would you personally find motivating?

- How is the context currently set up for using this habit? How can you influence the context?

- What systems can support using this habit? If you're using this for yourself as an individual, does the morning work for you personally or would a different time of day work better? Are you going to use this habit on the weekends or non-work days, and if so, what learning would you look to do?

- What one action will you start with, to begin implementing this habit for yourself?

Back to our story

At the beginning of this chapter, we mentioned that the pandemic shifted a family routine. For that family, with virtual schooling, they no longer needed to make lunches and get the girls out the door to the bus. The parents in that family had extra time in the morning. Before the pandemic, the father used to go to the gym, but with gyms closed, he started working out at home. The added convenience meant he ended up working out six days a week instead of his usual two to three times. Unlike many during the pandemic, he got in much better shape and continued this new routine even when gyms opened up again. And the mother in the family used the extra time in the morning to read more, and then she started writing more, and even built a website. This led to her finding a paid consulting engagement based on her research. The extra time in the morning just shifted their routine a little bit, but the changes added up over time. When schools returned to in person, the kids looked after their own lunches, and the parents were able to continue with their routines, just modified slightly.

This family's shift in routine was minor compared to so many families who suffered loss of income and struggled with young kids in virtual schooling. It wasn't a challenging shift in routine. I don't share this illustrative story as an example of a massive change, rather, I share this as an example of incremental change, shifting existing routines slightly, and adding learning and exercise in daily. It is far easier to shift existing routines slightly than to make a monumental shift.

Are there routines in your life that you could look to shift slightly? As you consider the habits in this book, look at the ones that would be a slight shift, rather than a monumental change, and start with those. Look for ways to start small and move to bigger things as you build success.

Key takeaways

- With this habit, learning becomes part of your everyday routine. Learning is done daily and integrated into the start of your day.

TABLE 15.1 Make the log-on learning habit AUTOMATIC

AUTOMATIC	Log-on learning habit ...
Allow for feeling good To get it done, make it fun.	Find learning materials that you enjoy and start with those.
Under the influence If the leader is a gem, we'll follow them.	Have a leader share what learning habits have worked for them – in a town hall, in a newsletter, blog post or otherwise.
Tip the scale If we can't see it, we often won't do it.	Have employees share what they are doing – capture their stories in a survey.
Ownership If it's mine, I think it's super fine.	Think of the learning time as your time; something that you are doing for yourself.
Mindset As a skill set grows, our fixed mindset will decompose.	Daily learning is for growth not remediation; focus on areas you want to build.

(continued)

TABLE 15.1 (Continued)

AUTOMATIC	Log-on learning habit ...
Avoid losses Don't ignore a potential gain just because a loss would be a pain.	Start small with the learning time and build on your success.
Towards the default To be quick, go with the default pick.	Add a learning site or resource to the start-up on your computer
Incentives A bird in the hand is worth two in the bush.	Give yourself a reward for daily learning – such as check it off a to-do list or keep a visible tally of days with learning, etc.
Commitment If I say it, I better do it.	Commit to daily learning in development plans or learning plans and share with someone.

References

Pink, D (2018) *When: The scientific secrets of perfect timing*, Riverhead Books, New York

Tong, M (2022) Global Director of Learning and Development [Interview] (2 May 2022)

Turner, S (2022) Global Head of Learning and Skills [Interview] (14 April 2022)

16

Follow-up actions

At a pharmaceutical company a few years ago, there were two colleagues in similar roles. They both used MS (Microsoft) Office for their work. Like many others at the company, they often needed to share files and work on documents with others. The company they worked for decided to offer Google Workspace for those that wanted to try it out for collaboration. The company offered courses on how to get started with using Google Workspace. Both colleagues, Tessa and Jackie, signed up for the courses and learned about Google Slides, Documents and Sheets.

After taking the courses, Tessa tried out the technology at work and played around with it. She thought about how it would help in her job and found a project where she could apply it and try it out. She chatted with co-workers about how they were using Google and they made suggestions that helped her use it as well. Slowly, her confidence in using the technology to share documents and collaborate with others increased.

Jackie took the same courses and had the same technology at her desk. She went back to her work and continued using the same office applications she was comfortable with. She felt it would slow her down to try out the new technology, so even when she needed to work with others on documents, she continued emailing versions and not collaborating online as Tessa was doing. Jackie felt the new technology might have made some of her work easier to do but she didn't spend a lot of time thinking about it; she had work to do.

Tessa and Jackie took the same courses but had different approaches with what to do afterwards and how to apply the learning. We'll hear more about how this turned out for them later in the chapter, but for now, let's dive into this habit.

Overview of the habit

Often, you may be doing some learning and you may be looking for ways to apply the learning in projects at work. Too often, employees keep learning and work separate and don't look for opportunities to apply the learning. The habit in this chapter can help you to seek out ways to apply the learning and help you find ways to use it in your work. You can first try out some of the new ideas or material in a safe space. You can think about how it could be applied in areas of your work. You can speak with others about the material. For example, your peers and your manager can be helpful partners in discussing what you're learning, how it applies, and where you could use the learning. The conversations alone will help you embed the learning as you will need to explain a bit of what you've been finding. And then actually applying the new skills at work will help you to further contextualize the learning and embed it within your existing mental models.

With this in mind, the habit for follow-up actions uses the contextual cue of being exposed to new tools, models or methods as the starting point. Then you can analyse ways to use the new material, try it out in a safe space, chat with others and apply the learning. This routine will reward you with feeling more confident in your learning, better prepared for the future, and it can also reward you with opportunities that wouldn't have been possible without the learning or speaking with your manager. Let's break it down specifically.

Cue

The cue for this habit is **that you are exposed to a new tool, technique or methodology and you learn about it.** This can happen through something you read, something you take in a course in a classroom or in an online course. This can happen through a conversation with a colleague where you learn something new. This could also be from a corporate initiative rolling out new technology. Or perhaps you have a project and you need to look up something to get a more efficient way of doing the project – for example, learning VLOOKUP or pivot tables in MS Excel in order to work with a data set more efficiently. There are lots of opportunities to learn something new. The difference with this habit is what routine you follow after you've been introduced to the new tool, technique or methodology.

Routine

Once you've been exposed to something new, you only get the benefit of it if you use it. **The routine for this habit is that you look for opportunities** to practise the new learning in a safe environment or you discuss it with a co-worker or manager and/or you look for opportunities to apply the new learning in your work and you update your methods to include the new learning. Without this routine following the learning, you will quickly forget what you learned or even if you remember it, you won't get the benefit of it as you are not using the new learning. It is key to solidify your learning by doing something with the learning – you need to try it out in order to embed the learning and update your mental models to include the new skills. If you keep the learning separate from the way you think about your work and your methods in working, then you are not embedding the new ideas into how you think and view your work (i.e. your mental model of your work), and this means you won't be using the new learning.

Reward

The reward for following this routine is that you can identify opportunities, based on the learning you've been doing, and the opportunities can make your work more interesting and/or rewarding. An additional reward is that by following this habit you will gain confidence in your abilities and feel better prepared as changes happen in the organization and in your work. You'll already be used to learning new ways of working and applying new ideas, so when organizational changes happen or when technology changes your work, you'll be more confident and prepared to adjust and see opportunities.

Context

This habit helps to build and maintain the context that learning and looking for opportunities to apply the learning are part of the social norms of your work. By doing this habit regularly, including speaking with others about your learning and discussing how it can apply in the organizational context, it affects the social norms of your peer network, showing that learning is done and discussed regularly. In this way, even though it is an individual habit, it helps to build innovation and new ideas throughout your network because it uses your peers and manager as part of the habit.

FIGURE 16.1 Follow-up actions habit

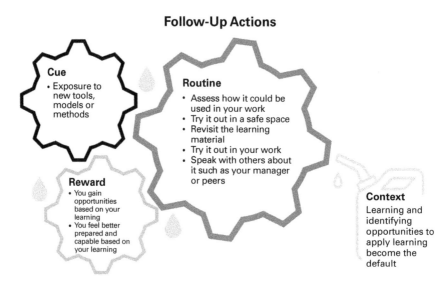

Measurement for the habit

To track your progress on this habit, here are some simple measurements you can look at to see how you're doing and perhaps to establish or change your goals for what you will achieve.

You can measure this habit by checking:

- Amount of learning you are doing – number of articles read, number of courses completed, number of books read, number of podcasts listened to, number of learning videos watched.
  - You can use a visual to help track this – something as simple as a tally on a piece of paper displayed at your desk or more formally in a tracking document online.
- Amount of time you are spending learning – set a target, add the time blocks to your calendar and then check back if you completed the learning you targeted.
- Amount of time you spend trying out the learning – when you practise it or use it on a project.
- Percentage of learning that you apply in your work or try out in a safe environment – i.e. read article then tried it out = 100 per cent.
- Number of conversations with your manager about learning and opportunities and frequency of those conversations – once per month, once every two months, etc.
- Number of peers you discussed learning with and how often did you discuss learning with them.
- Number of opportunities uncovered.
- Number of opportunities achieved.

For the above measurements, you could use something called an Archer's Mindset. This is an idea Annie Duke shares in her book *How to Decide* (Duke, 2020). The idea with an Archer's Mindset is to set a target for yourself and then to try to get as close as possible to the target. If you think of an archer's target, even if you don't hit bullseye, you could still be on the board, and it was still worth the shot. This is the type of mindset to use when setting targets for yourself, so that you don't consider it a failure if you don't hit the target exactly or get a bullseye every time, but rather that it's a good idea to have an idea of where you want to land and work to get as close as possible to that spot.

Make it AUTOMATIC

A – Allow for feeling good. Make learning fun for yourself by finding a quick reward that works for you and using it. For example, some people like to mark things off as completed on their to-do lists. You could use this with your calendar by marking the learning time or practice time complete on your calendar. Or for applying the learning, reward yourself with a quick break after trying out something new that you've learned. Find something that works for you to make the process enjoyable.

U – Under the Influence. Find out about how leaders in your organization learn and how they apply their learning. This can help you in your own learning, and you can use their example in conversations when seeking out opportunities to apply learning, especially in conversations with your manager. Finding someone who has successfully applied learning, and who you can relate to, can help provide an example and context for your own learning at work.

T – Tip the scale. Pair up with a partner to help your learning. We learn better and stick to our goals more when we have a partner to hold us accountable. When you have a partner at work to discuss learning with, and help each other, you will both achieve your goals better, and you'll learn more by having the opportunity to discuss your learning and put it in the work context, with a peer. Learning on your own can be effective, but when you share the learning with a partner, it is even more effective for both of you. You can broaden this further by discussing what you're learning with your network. New ideas can come from conversations and by speaking about what you're learning; it can help you structure thoughts and test your assumptions.

O – Ownership. As you decide what to learn, think about your current skill set and what areas look like opportunities or things you're interested in learning more about. You don't need to have a massive change in mind when you start using this habit, just nudge your current skill set along a little bit, do it regularly; and then over time it will make for a big change. And that change will be based on your interests and ideas, which will make it all the more rewarding because it is unique to you.

M – Mindset. With your learning, if you are struggling to think of ways to try out the learning or apply it in your work, challenge yourself to think of one thing you could do to apply the learning. You may want to chat with a co-worker or your team to get ideas for how to apply the learning. Often people struggle with how new ideas fit into their own work, so challenge yourself to think of one, even small, way to apply the learning. Once you get started, other ideas and applications will appear. By finding one way, you'll open up the possibilities for growth.

A – Avoid losses. As you spend time on learning and follow-up, remind yourself of the benefits of this approach. You may be tempted to just think of the time you are spending on learning as a loss of time, as often we focus on negatives, but instead think of your habit anatomy design and what rewards you had listed. In this way, you'll focus on the benefits and train your thinking to expand your learning rather than having a scarcity mindset and focusing on any potential losses.

T – Towards the default. For learning and follow-up, block the time in your calendar on a recurring basis so that the time is already allocated and you need to actively move it to change the plan. In this way, the learning time and learning follow-up becomes the default and it becomes easier to follow the default rather than change it. The calendar blocks will also serve as a visual reminder to support your implementation intentions.

I – Incentives. With your learning, you may be working towards a larger goal that is further off – such as a certification or a promotion. Be sure to reward yourself along the way to help you stick with the habit. Give yourself a five-minute break after completing a learning task; let yourself spend a few minutes checking social media or reading something fun as a quick reward. Working towards a bigger goal is made a lot easier if you have small rewards along the way, so find something that works for you and use it to keep on track.

C – Commitment. We know we're more likely to stick with a goal or a commitment if we share it with others, so ensure you are holding yourself accountable by articulating your plan and then sharing it with someone else. You could share your plan with your accountability partner or the peer you are working on learning with; you could share your plan with your manager or someone else that will help you stick with your plan. The main thing is to commit to the plan and hold yourself accountable by sharing your commitment with someone else.

YOUR ACTION PLAN

To make this habit your own, consider the following strategies:

- Do you have an existing cue for this habit? If not, consider booking a recurring meeting with yourself for learning and planning your follow-up actions.

- Do you want to speak with your manager about learning and opportunities or is there someone else that you would rather talk to about this? Perhaps a colleague or a mentor?

- Does the routine work for you? How would you adjust it to work better for your style?

- Are there other rewards you are aiming for? For example, is there some specific learning goal or opportunity that you are working towards? Update the reward in the habit to what you are looking to achieve – and be sure to celebrate small successes along the way.

- Does your current context support the use of this habit? For example, do others in your network already discuss their learning and ideas for applying the learning? If your colleagues are not in this habit, consider starting it to spark their interest in also learning and following up on learning. If you think this wouldn't fit well with your colleagues, then consider seeking out a group where it would fit – perhaps on a project team or in collaboration with other departments.

With the above considerations and AUTOMATIC suggestions, how will you move forward with this habit? What is your next step?

Back to our story

At the beginning of our chapter we heard about Tessa and Jackie. They both took the same course, but afterwards, Tessa used the new technology and Jackie continued working the way she had before being introduced to the new technology.

When Tessa played around with the new technology, it took her a lot longer to complete a project than Jackie who went back to doing the project the way she'd done it in the past. But then Tessa got the hang of the new collaboration technology. The next project she was faster than before, still not as quick as Jackie but getting faster. She played with the new technology some more and got better with it. Tessa continued doing what she'd been doing. The next project Tessa was faster than she had been before. And she was able to find more efficiencies by understanding the new collaboration capabilities. She mentioned these in a team meeting. The team began to collaborate using the new tools as well and benefitted from the increased efficiencies.

Jackie, on the other hand, did not change how she'd been working. Even when people shared documents with her in the new tools, she would convert them to the versions she was used to and continue her work as she had before. Soon Tessa got a reputation for being open and collaborative, and when a team lead position opened up, she was promoted. Jackie, however, continued working as she had done and began to get a reputation as not being open to change. When there was a restructure in the firm, Tessa was further promoted and Jackie struggled to fit into the new structure.

This story is fictional but it illustrates the power of being open to learning and applying the learning. This habit can open up new opportunities and it is valuable in helping shape your mindset so that you can adapt and change as changes happen in the workplace.

Key takeaways

- When we learn something, if we don't apply it, the learning is often lost. In order to remember and use what you have learned, follow this habit of follow-up actions to find opportunities to apply your learning and adjust it for your needs

- By using the learning in this way, your work will be more interesting and you will uncover opportunities that you may not have expected.

TABLE 16.1 Make the follow-up actions habit AUTOMATIC

AUTOMATIC	Follow-up actions habit ...
Allow for feeling good To get it done, make it fun.	Celebrate the small successes along the way – mark yourself as complete on your learning time blocks or give yourself a short mental break after you complete a learning block.
Under the influence If the leader is a gem, we'll follow them.	Seek out leaders in your organization who talk about their learning and how they applied it – reference these people when speaking with your manager and in planning your learning.
Tip the scale If we can't see it, we often won't do it.	Pair up with a colleague to both learn and both discuss with your managers – add a check-in with each other to hold each other accountable.
Ownership If it's mine, I think it's super fine.	Recognize your current skill set and reward yourself as you continue to build it.
Mindset As a skill set grows, our fixed mindset will decompose.	If you can't think of ways to apply the learning, challenge yourself to rethink how you are thinking of your learning and work. Start small and build on your success.
Avoid losses Don't ignore a potential gain just because a loss would be a pain.	When blocking time for learning and follow up – remind yourself of the benefits you'll see by following through on your commitment to yourself.
Towards the default To be quick, go with the default pick.	Use the power of going with the default by putting learning time and follow up blocks on your calendar.
Incentives A bird in the hand is worth two in the bush.	Give yourself small rewards when you complete a milestone or achieve one of your measurement targets.
Commitment If I say it, I better do it.	Hold yourself accountable to your commitments – and help yourself achieve this by sharing your plans with others.

References

Duke, A (2020) *How to Decide: Simple tools for making better choices*, Portfolio, New York

Tong, M (2022) Interview about learning habits in organizations [Interview] (2 May 2022)

17

Collaboration channel

A few years ago a company implemented a collaboration tool with channels for employees to discuss work. There were channels for organizational groups, divisions and teams, and channels for subject areas that allowed cross-functional team members to discuss various topics and projects. The channels varied in how much they were used. But one team had a very active channel of their own with great engagement. That team also reported higher engagement at work and had a lower attrition rate than comparable teams. How did that team use their channel in a way that supported engagement? We'll hear more about that later but first let's look at this habit.

Overview of the habit

The collaboration channel habit involves sharing ideas and new materials in a team collaboration channel, sparked by recent learning. This habit helps the team innovate and learn from each other, and encourages engagement and new ideas. Often learning is siloed and, if shared, only done so via one-on-one conversations or more formally in team meetings. If learning is only shared in one-on-one conversations, then strong partnerships can build together but the rest of the team may fall behind, as they aren't getting the benefit of the shared collaboration and innovation.

Teams can share insights in team meetings, which is a key learning habit that we looked at in Chapter 12. To further enhance team sharing, a collaboration channel is a great way to extend this collaboration between meetings and support those who may have missed the meeting. Rather than relying on people to look up the meeting recording or find materials in emails, a collaboration channel can support and extend the discussion to benefit the team between meetings.

The collaboration channel method of sharing ideas, asking questions or sharing new materials can encourage learning as team members can post as soon as they have a new idea or learning sparks a question, which builds momentum for fledgling ideas. The channel also provides an archive of discussions that can be searched and referenced later, making it easy to go back to something from earlier. This is faster than searching through meeting recordings or emails. In addition, the less formal nature of sharing in a collaboration channel can encourage more team members to react and engage, which then encourages people to post and share more.

This collaboration channel habit is one way of supporting continuous learning and helping to drive innovation – and can be used in combination with other methods to help you better understand what you're learning and apply new learning in your role, and help the team innovate and collaborate together.

Cue

The cue for this habit is learning something that has sparked a new idea, a question or provided the inspiration for a new tool or an enhancement to an existing tool. As you're taking a course, reading an article, browsing a book or trying out a hands-on exercise as part of a learning programme, you'll think of questions, and get new ideas and thoughts on how to apply the learning in your role. Some people like to keep notes as they are learning so they can gather and solidify their thoughts, and you can mark your learning ideas with a special character to make new ideas stand out from your other notes.

For example, when I'm reading a book, I keep a notebook handy and note down the page number of interesting quotes or ideas from the book, and I mark my thoughts and ideas with the word idea circled like this: (Idea) This helps me when reviewing my notes to find the ideas that were sparked by my reading, and then use them or build on them.

Routine

The routine for this habit following the cue above, is that you post in a collaboration channel and share your question, idea, new tools or other items related to your learning. This will help you integrate your learning into how you work and, by sharing it in a collaboration channel, it will not only help you solidify your thoughts, but it will benefit others in their learning as well. The collaboration chat resulting from your post can also help you to better articulate your ideas, or provide inspiration and innovation as a group. The questions that others ask will help you refine your ideas, or the new tools you've created, to make them even better. And by sharing this in a group channel, the team gets the benefit of learning together, in a way that is recorded and searchable for later as needed.

Reward

The reward for this habit for you is that you get instant feedback through the comments and reactions that your team shares in response to your post. You can also get **recognition for collaborating and sharing new ideas,** which is often something that is looked at in performance metrics. On a side note, because the channel is recorded and searchable, you can reference the number of posts and items shared in your performance review, as needed. The biggest reward from this habit is the peer collaboration because it is often through discussion with peers that we solidify our ideas and take items we've learned and turn them into ways we can use them in our roles. Teams that collaborate in this way also tend to be more creative and engaging, making work more enjoyable for everyone and showing in metrics like reduced attrition and higher engagement scores. By participating in this habit, you are helping yourself and making your team a better place to work.

Context

The context for this habit is that the team collaborates about learning and ideas. By everyone posting, and commenting and reacting to each other's posts, it encourages a social norm of collaboration and safety in sharing new ideas. This is very important for this habit to work. While each individual needs to post and react to other posts, it is the team, as a whole, all doing this that supports this habit on an ongoing basis. If no one comments when people post, then the number of posts will soon decline and dwindle. The team, as a whole, needs to support each other in this habit, and then the team as a group will get the benefits of this habit.

FIGURE 17.1 Collaboration channel habit

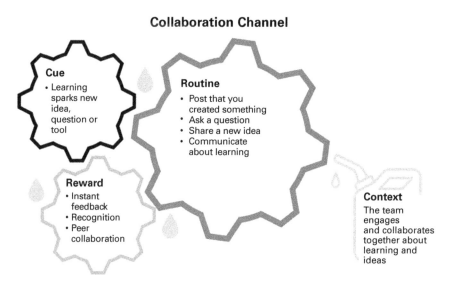

Collaboration Channel

Cue
• Learning sparks new idea, question or tool

Routine
• Post that you created something
• Ask a question
• Share a new idea
• Communicate about learning

Reward
• Instant feedback
• Recognition
• Peer collaboration

Context
The team engages and collaborates together about learning and ideas

Measurement for the habit

As you look at using this habit for yourself, you can measure your progress by looking at some of these metrics. You can do this informally to get yourself into the habit of posting, by setting a goal for yourself for how many posts you'll do and getting into the habit of reacting to other people's posts. You can also set expectations for yourself on how often you check the channel. By using these metrics informally, you can have your own idea of what good looks like, so you can work towards achieving that for yourself. So checking:

- the team channel at least once per day
- number of times shared a new idea per month on average
- number of times asked a question per month
- number of posts sharing a tool you created or you found, per month, on average
- number of posts responded to per week or per month
- number of team members whose posts you responded to per week or per month (to look at distribution across the team)

If you are a leader and you would like to encourage your team to use this habit, here are some metrics you can consider to informally see if you and your team are using this habit in the way that you want:

- number of posts the team shares per day or per week
- average number of reactions or comments per post by team across what number of team members
- number of posts that you comment or react to as manager
- team responsiveness on posts – time elapsed from post to comment on average
- manager responsiveness on posts – time elapsed from post to manager comment or reaction on average

This combination of metrics will help you set what you consider to be good for this habit for yourself or for your team. You'll want to balance responsiveness with the perception of an expectation that everyone reacts immediately, which would mean you may interrupt your work too frequently to post or comment. You'll also want to balance your comments on your team's posts, and ensure you all collaborate together and that those who post less often are encouraged by comments and reactions from the group. You can make the habit your own and help to establish the expectations for the team by participating. If you're the manager, you may even want to clarify expectations and explain this habit so that your team, especially new team members, all understand what's expected and know why people are posting and what's expected.

There are a number of metrics suggested here, but that doesn't mean the expectation is that you would use them all. The list is meant to be suggestions that you can consider and then pick what might work for you. And you can revisit the list over time and consider other ones, especially as the habit grows.

Make it AUTOMATIC

A – Allow for feeling good. Collaboration channels can really help to make work more fun. When you're posting to share a new idea, something you created, something you learned or to ask a question, keep your post engaging. If you can use emojis or gifs, it will make your post more likely to get engagement from your group. Pictures and icons make the text more interesting and will encourage others to react and comment, which helps everyone. You'll want to use a thread or sub-discussion to get deeper into the topic, rather than filling up the main channel. But, overall, the idea is to make your post engaging and enticing to others, to encourage them to participate in the chat. This will help everyone build on each other's ideas and collaborate more effectively.

U – Under the influence. Check out how your manager posts in the channel. If you're the manager for the group, comment on posts and be encouraging. This will help set the tone and encourage others to post as well. Often, the group will look to the leader of the group for how to post in a group collaboration channel, so be sure to set a tone that encourages the group to collaborate effectively, and that will encourage the group to share new ideas and things they've created, to the channel.

T – Tip the scale. You may want to just share an update one-on-one with someone or in a conversation in a meeting, which is a good way to share as well. But by sharing ideas, innovative solutions and asking questions in a group channel, it allows everyone to benefit and encourages the group as a whole to share. When you share just one-on-one, others miss out on the benefits of ideas and collaboration. Consider if your post would also help others in the group chat and share accordingly.

O – Ownership. For group discussions and collaboration, the size of the group matters. While large groups for big divisions are useful for posts that affect the larger audience, often it's nice to share new ideas or try things out in a smaller setting. That's why a collaboration channel for direct team members is important and provides a space that is just for that group to collaborate. For new ideas or tools created, the smaller group can serve as an incubator before items are shared with bigger groups.

M – Mindset. Some people are hesitant to post in a group collaboration channel as they are worried what others will think of their post or that they will say the wrong thing, or that others won't be interested. That's where just starting small and trying it out can help. Posts can be edited after they are posted, so if you don't get it right the first time or don't like how it looks after you've posted, you can edit it. Collaboration is to share ideas and engage with the group, so just try it out and edit along the way.

A – Avoid losses. You may be concerned about a loss of face or that people won't be interested in what you post. Start by commenting and reacting to other people's posts, this will help set the social norms for the group and encourage others to comment and react. Then just try out posting yourself and maybe tag people for their insight or comments as needed. As with the mindset note above, remember you can edit your posts, so if you don't like it once it's posted, change it.

T – Towards the default. Collaboration channels make it easy to react to other people's posts without having to write anything yourself. If someone else reacts with an emoji, you can just click on it as well to add on. Or you can add an emoji yourself. This makes it easy to engage without having to write out a comment yourself, and it will encourage people to share. If you're not sure what to say, just use the emojis to get started.

I – Incentives. Collaboration channels at work are similar to social media posts – often the reward is getting comments or reactions from your peers. The reactions and comments can serve as an incentive to keep going. Remember this when others post so you can help encourage them as well. And when you share something that you think will help the team, getting their reactions and comments can serve as incentive to keep going.

C – Commitment. Sharing in a collaboration channel can help you continue with learning and creating – you'll get questions from people on what you've created or learned that will help you understand your ideas better, and apply them in your roles. You'll get questions or feedback on the materials that you create that will help you make them better. The channel serves as a public commitment to learning and building that will help you continue in your learning habits.

YOUR ACTION PLAN

To begin with this habit, you'll want to consider how you learn and how you think about new ideas and new tools as you learn. This will help form the cue for your use of this habit so think about what you're currently doing and how you can use it as a cue to post in a collaboration channel.

Consider how you post now and if there's any part of the routine suggested here that you'll want to modify for your own use. As you consider this, think about the reward of posting – do you find you're encouraged to post when others comment on your posts or react to what you've shared? Do you find it helpful to post questions? Do you find that your team is responsive and if not, is there a way you can encourage everyone to be more responsive? What is the expectation about monitoring channels and is it helpful or a little overwhelming? Consider this as you look at what you think will be good for you in using this habit, and have a look at the measurements to see if there are any, that even informally, you could look at to see if you are using this habit in the way that you want.

As you continue or begin using this habit, think about the context of your team channel – does it support collaboration and learning and if not, what would help to shift the context so that it is part of the way the team works?

Having considered your own modifications of your cue, routine, reward and context for this habit, now decide on what your one next step will be to get started with this habit.

Back to our story

What was different about the team that had more engagement over-all and a lower attrition rate? Their team regularly posted in their channel. They posted about events and regular updates just like other teams, but what was different was that all team members posted to share things they'd learned or new tools they had created or discovered. And when they posted, the other team members very quickly reacted to the posts with comments or emojis. The manager of the team was usually the first to post, and responded with enthusiastic comments that came through in text. The team members followed suit and commented as well.

The team became known for innovation, sharing and collaboration. In other teams, where there was little reaction to posts, it meant that fewer and fewer people posted, and when they did, they often didn't get any response, so gradually the interaction faded. The engaged team used the collaboration channel to enhance the innovation, sharing and learning across the team. This was especially helpful as the team was fully remote. Everyone did better in their roles and the team was more successful in hitting their targets together.

Key takeaways

- Collaboration channels can provide a searchable group forum for learning reflection and ideas.
- Sharing ideas and new tools in one-on-one discussions and team meetings can be enhanced across the team by using a collaboration channel as well.
- The team needs to support each other by not only posting themselves, but also commenting and reacting to team members posts.

TABLE 17.1 Make the collaboration channel habit AUTOMATIC

AUTOMATIC	Collaboration channel habit ...
Allow for feeling good To get it done, make it fun.	Add emojis or fun gifs to your post and make your tone friendly. React to other people's posts with emojis and encouraging comments.
Under the influence If the leader is a gem, we'll follow them.	The leader in your channel sets the tone, so as a leader, comment and reply when team members post and encourage others to do the same.
Tip the scale If we can't see it, we often won't do it.	A collaboration channel shares updates with the group instead of in one-on-one messages. Consider sharing updates in group channels so more people can benefit.
Ownership If it's mine, I think it's super fine.	Use a collaboration channel for your direct team, so the group is small enough to be comfortable posting. If your team doesn't have a channel, consider setting one up.
Mindset As a skill set grows, our fixed mindset will decompose.	Unlike emails, posts can be edited even after they're posted; so if you don't like what you post, you can change it after. Just keep trying.
Avoid losses Don't ignore a potential gain just because a loss would be a pain.	If you're concerned others won't be interested in what you post; try it out and see what kind of reaction you get. Comment on other people's posts so you can help set the group norms.
Towards the default To be quick, go with the default pick.	If someone else posts and you're not sure what to comment, just click an emoji reaction or like the post.
Incentives A bird in the hand is worth two in the bush.	As you begin posting and sharing, the reactions and comments from your peers can serve as an incentive to continue.
Commitment If I say it, I better do it.	By posting about new ideas or sharing something you've created, others will encourage you to use what you have created, and you'll get new ideas to build further.

18

Accountability partner

When I graduated with a Bachelor of Arts focused on history, I wasn't quite sure what career to get into. I started working in financial services and explored some courses in the evenings, but I wasn't interested or engaged to continue. Then I started a programme focused on adult learning that could lead to a second degree. The programme involved going to class every second Saturday, which at the time was feasible for me. To graduate from the programme, you had to take a number of courses and from the pace I was taking them it would take about two and half years to do the programme, which seemed quite daunting when I started.

In the first class, the professor shared a number of study tips. I had been out of school for a number of years at this point so I found the tips very helpful. She recommended bibliographic software that allows you to keep track of what you've read, then find and insert references into your writing quickly and easily. She recommended a quick format for note-taking when reading research – note down the key takeaways with page numbers, why the research is relevant, how it could be applied in the context of our own practice and what further research is needed. And she encouraged us to engage with others in the class. One of her recommendations made a massive difference to my success in the programme. And it's a fairly simple one. That brings us to our next habit.

Overview of the habit

When we have a goal, if we work towards it on our own, we have a 10 to 25 per cent chance of achieving our goal. If we share our plan with someone else, our chance of success rises to 65 per cent. If we meet with the person and discuss our progress on the goal, our chance of success rises to 95 per cent (Kander, 2022). That is a much better chance of success, so how does this work exactly?

Pairing up and sharing a goal, then holding each other accountable is called an accountability partner, our next habit. An accountability partner or learning partner is someone that you pair up with and you both hold each other accountable for your goals. You meet regularly to discuss your progress, talk through obstacles, discuss how your learning applies to your goals and work, discuss new ideas and support each other as you work through your learning. This will help you not only achieve more in your learning, but it makes the process of learning more enjoyable and engaging as you have a peer to help you along the way.

Cue

The cue for this habit is to have a regular, recurring meeting with each other. When you're in a course together, this can be the in-class course that is already a recurring meeting. But in the context of continuous learning where there is no scheduled class, the cue for this habit is a regular recurring meeting on your calendars. This can be 15 minutes weekly or it can be 30 minutes every two weeks, or a cadence that suits you both. The important thing is that it is regular and recurring so that you connect to discuss your learning and you both have the time set aside to meet and share ideas. If you leave it to be scheduled ad hoc or when you can fit it in, it won't happen and this won't be a habit, and your chances of success with your goals will drop accordingly.

Routine

The routine for this habit is that you discuss your learning and help each other. When you meet, you check-in on progress towards goals, discuss your learning, how you're finding it, how it applies in your work, and then you both decide on what your next action will be – what will you get done before you meet again. In this way, your conversations will help you both achieve your goals, and will help you both better understand your learning and contextualize it. This is a very important step in learning as you need to embed your learning in your own mental models, your way of thinking and seeing the world, and when you are learning you need to integrate what you have learned into your way of thinking. Your accountability partner, along with the other individual habits outlined in this book, can be an important component of how you do that.

Reward

The reward for this partnership for both people is that you have support while you are learning and increase your chances of achieving your goals. Through the peer collaboration, feedback and encouragement, you will both benefit and have a much greater chance at success in your endeavours. The process of meeting up and chatting about learning has many other benefits too – the social support and comradery that can develop, exposure to new ideas and new ways of thinking – these are benefits that you would not have had alone. When we go to a class for learning, partnerships of this nature may happen organically. When you are in a continuous learning environment with no scheduled classes, you need to be intentional about seeking a partner and helping each other.

Context

We know from AUTOMATIC that people feel they should continue with their commitments if they have shared those commitments with others, as we like to be consistent and hold a consistent view of ourselves. This supports the context for the efficacy of having an accountability partner. It creates an environment for us to share our commitments and hold each other accountable, which supports us in achieving our goals. This context is important, especially when learning something new or where we may be feeling a sense of inadequacy

FIGURE 18.1 Accountability partner habit

Accountability Partner

Cue
- Recurring invite for 30 minutes bi-weekly to connect

Routine
- Check in on what's happened since last met
- Discuss progress on goals
- Share how applying learning
- Commit to next action

Reward
- Peer collaboration
- Encouragement
- Feedback

Context
Supportive environment to continue with commitments

as we get out of our comfort zone and try new ways of thinking and doing things through learning. The supportive context of having someone with us as we go through this process is very important.

Measurement for the habit

To hold yourself accountable on your use of this habit, you can consider the following metrics. These metrics are also helpful to discuss with your accountability partner so that you are on the same page about your cadence of meeting and how you will structure your partnership. You don't need to be super formal when chatting about this but it's good to both articulate your expectations so that you can come to an agreement on how you'll work together. Have a look through the list of metrics below and think about your idea of how these would play out, then chat with your partner so that you come to an agreement. And, of course, as things change and your partnership evolves, you can adjust.

Consider the following metrics:

- Frequency of meeting – weekly, bi-weekly, monthly.
- Number of times met – are you meeting regularly or are meetings cancelled/rescheduled a lot?
- Time spent meeting – will you check in with each other for 15 minutes every week, 30 minutes every second week? A different cadence?
- Number of times met in person – is it possible to meet in person? How often?
- Number of cancellations – what is acceptable?
- Number of reschedules – what is acceptable?

Make a plan for what will work for both of you. It can be as simple as setting the recurring invite and then if meetings get rescheduled two to three times, checking if you need to change the timeslot. If meetings get cancelled three or more times with no reschedule, maybe consider if the partnership structure is working.

Make it AUTOMATIC

A – Allow for feeling good. Formally partnering as accountability partners and setting up a recurring invite can feel a bit stiff and perhaps awkward, especially if you don't know the person well or you've been asked to find a partner to pair up with by a programme you're in or by your manager. Regardless, the experience can still be engaging and enjoyable so make sure to set that tone when you chat – your discussions can hold each other accountable and be enjoyable at the same time.

U – Under the influence. When you're choosing a partner, if possible, seek out someone you admire and would like to know better. You can both support each other and hold each other accountable, and in bringing different strengths to the partnership you can both learn from each other. If you already admire the person and want to learn from them, you'll get more out of the partnership as you start.

T – Tip the scale. Often, groups or teams decide to use accountability partners as a strategy for their group. In this case, it's helpful to hear how the rest of the group is doing with accountability partners – for example, in a team meeting sharing how it's going for one pair can help the other pairs to continue or reignite with their recurring meetings. If you're part of a group or team that are using accountability partners, check in to see how others are doing with their partnerships to get ideas and inspiration. And if your partnership is something you set up outside of a group, then periodically ask around to find others who use this strategy, and find out how it is going or what works or doesn't work.

O – Ownership. When you're pairing up in a partnership, make sure both of you will get something out of the pairing. Discuss this up front and then check in periodically to make sure the accountability partnership is still working for both of you and adjust as needed. This is a pairing that should be beneficial to both of you, and things change over time, so you'll need to check in on how each of you are finding things to stay aligned. You may want to set a timeframe for the partnership and then discuss extending when you reach that point, to make it easy to keep going or change this up when needed.

M – Mindset. The partnership will work best if you are both open to new ideas and support from the other person. Keep a growth mindset at the forefront as you discuss ideas so that you both have the opportunity to integrate new ideas into what you're doing. It's good to have a growth mindset framework in your thoughts as you may find yourself feeling defensive or unable to integrate new learning because of fixed mental models that you don't even realize are underlying your way of thinking; so being open to articulating your point of view so that you can recognize it and be open to changing your way of thinking, will help you get the most out of your learning and the partnership.

A – Avoid losses. It may feel like a burden to keep a recurring meeting on your calendar and stick with the timeslot to meet. Keep it short and frequent to just quickly check in and discuss your committed actions. When this accountability partner strategy is tied to a programme that is already scheduled (such as a weekly class) it doesn't feel like something extra to spend the time talking with your partner. With a shift to continuous learning, you need to schedule the time separately and that can feel like you're losing time from other things you need to be doing. But as part of your growth plan and learning, an accountability partner can be a key component of reaching your goals, and make getting there more enjoyable, so keep quick check-ins frequent and enjoyable.

T – Towards the default. When you establish a partnership and decide on your check-in cadence, send a meeting invite and make it recurring. This way it is on both your calendars by default. If you leave it as something you book, and then book the next one when you speak etc, it will be too easy to lack a cadence and you are at risk of letting the meeting fall off your calendar.

I – Incentives. If you and your partner are located near each other, consider getting together in person either regularly or occasionally. If you can meet for coffee or for lunch sometimes, that will provide an incentive to get together.

C – Commitment. Use the partnership to hold each other accountable and be intentional about this. Consider sharing one action that you will commit to completing before your next meeting, and then start off your next check in by sharing how that action went and if you completed it. If you both do this it will be an easy way to structure your discussions and it will serve as a trigger to hold you each accountable.

YOUR ACTION PLAN

To begin with this habit you'll want to find a partner who is interested in working to support each other on your goals. You may want to seek out someone who is learning about the same things as you, perhaps with the same overall timeframe. Get together to discuss how you could pair up and help you each achieve your goals. Then you'll need to decide on the parameters that work for both of you, including:

- How and when will you meet?
- Where will you meet – virtual or in person, and if in person, where?

- How long will your check-ins be?

- What format will you use for your check-ins?

- How long will you continue to meet? Is there a natural end point based on each person's goals (i.e. achieving a certification, finishing a programme of material)?

- Who will send the invite?

After you've been meeting for a little while, check in on how things are progressing for the partnership. Is it still working for you both, do you need to change anything? Review the AUTOMATIC suggestions to ensure you are on track with making this a habit and beneficial for you both. Celebrate achieving your goals and milestones as you progress. If you find the partnership helpful, tell others how this worked for you so you can help tip the scale for them and encourage others.

Back to our story

As you will have guessed by now, one of the suggestions that my professor made in that programme was that we pair up with a learning partner. She asked us to pair up in the class and ask each other a few questions, then we had to introduce our partner to the class and they would introduce us. Through that process, I met Angela. We both worked in corporate training. We got to know each other throughout the courses in the programme, and one more person, Darrin, joined our group as his partner left the programme. The three of us did many projects together, we met for lunches outside of class, we discussed our learning and our careers, and what our plans were. Through our partnership, we were all successful with the programme. We all graduated with the bachelor degree focused on adult education. Sitting in class near the end of the programme, I remember wondering if I would continue on with my studies and do a Master's degree. I had been very hesitant in the past to consider graduate school as it seemed like an overwhelming endeavour. And I remember having a sudden realization, that because I had these friends now, because that's what they had become, that I had the support to continue, that I should seize this moment as I had the ability, the time and now the social support to continue with my studies. It is thanks to having accountability partners that I continued on to complete a Master of Education focused on learning, work and change. Darrin and Angela also continued on to do graduate studies. For myself, if I hadn't got into the habit of having a learning partner, to discuss our studies, figure out how things applied, support each other when work was getting tough, I would not have continued on. And you wouldn't be reading about this experience in this book, as I probably wouldn't have written the book. An accountability partner can make learning so much more engaging and it can help you both to be more successful than you would be alone. It can be life changing.

Key takeaways

- An accountability partner is someone you pair up with to hold each other accountable and support each other in learning.
- With continuous learning, it's important to be intentional about meeting regularly with your accountability partner for check-ins with each other to discuss your mutual progress towards goals.

TABLE 18.1 Make the accountability partner habit AUTOMATIC

AUTOMATIC	Accountability partner habit ...
Allow for feeling good To get it done, make it fun.	Pick an accountability partner that you want to chat with so that you look forward to connecting.
Under the influence If the leader is a gem, we'll follow them.	Consider joining a mentorship program to connect with a leader you admire as an accountability partner.

(continued)

TABLE 18.1 (Continued)

AUTOMATIC	Accountability partner habit ...
Tip the scale If we can't see it, we often won't do it.	Suggest that your team joins you in having accountability partners and include a brief update on how it's going in team meetings periodically.
Ownership If it's mine, I think it's super fine.	Pair up with someone where you will both get value from meeting and commit to partnering together.
Mindset As a skill set grows, our fixed mindset will decompose.	Be open to new ideas and feedback from your partner as you learn. If you feel yourself becoming defensive, consider if you're using a fixed mindset.
Avoid losses Don't ignore a potential gain just because a loss would be a pain.	Remember the benefits of meeting with your partner – and adjust the time and cadence to what works better for you both.
Towards the default To be quick, go with the default pick.	Book a recurring meeting so it is on both your calendars.
Incentives A bird in the hand is worth two in the bush.	Consider meeting for coffee or lunch occasionally with your partner, instead of virtual meetings, if possible.
Commitment If I say it, I better do it.	Agree to commit to one action each at the end of every meeting, and then check in on progress at the start of the next sync.

Reference

Kander, D (2022) 3 strategies for holding yourself accountable, *Harvard Business Review*. [online] https://hbr.org/2022/02/3-strategies-for-holding-yourself-accountable (archived at https://perma.cc/9DTA-RFJB)

19

Conversations

During your career, have you ever worked at a company where people were open to chatting about new ideas, where people would share new insights and talk about new learning, across departments and within teams? How did that feel? How did you enjoy working there? And have you ever worked at a firm or on a team where the opposite was true? Where people didn't discuss new ideas or if they did, if someone brought up a new idea, or shared a new finding, it was generally negatively received? How did that lack of sharing ideas feel? Often, a lack of cross-pollination of ideas within teams and across departments can make work less interesting. It can be very demotivating and may negatively impact the results of the company.

At one company before 2020, there was a technical team that shared new ideas. If someone read an article or had an interesting discussion that sparked a new way of doing things, they would share it with others on their team. The team was bursting with posts in their collaboration channels; they had a section during their team meeting to share new ideas, resources or bring up fresh insights. And each team member informally contributed to this sharing culture by actively seeking out others to bounce ideas around and discuss what they'd learned recently. Which brings us to our topic in this chapter.

Overview of the habit

The conversations learning habit consists of chatting with others about learning. The benefit is that you will understand the learning better, and it can make work more engaging for both you and the people in your conversation network.

When you learn something new, do you chat about it with other people? We looked at the habit of having an accountability partner, but this chapter is about conversations – casual conversations with various people.

Casual conversations with others can help us to understand what we are learning and think of ways to apply it. If you were in a classroom session, this would be an obvious component of interacting with others in the class. But when it comes to continuous learning, where people are learning different things at different times, conversations are often an overlooked and underrated activity that gets missed.

Conversations help you to clarify your thinking as you explain your thoughts on the learning to someone else, and discussing it casually will help you to understand and apply new concepts. The conversations do not have to be a formal thing, just chatting before or after a meeting can be helpful, or when you go for coffee or lunch with someone. This isn't a formal accountability partner, it's not a mentor, just chatting about learning with various people can help you better understand what you are learning and think of ways to apply it to your situation and your role.

Cue

The cue for this habit is learning something new. After you've listened to a podcast, read an article, done a course or any other source of learning, that's the cue for starting this habit and seeking out an opportunity to chat about the learning.

Routine

The routine for this habit is to reach out to a colleague and chat about a new idea, tool or technique, based on your recent learning,

and discussing how it might work in the context of your roles, and what adjustments might be needed to make it work in your environment. During the casual conversation, you can explain what you found and your current thinking on it, and bounce ideas around with the person you are chatting with.

In your conversation, you can discuss if it might fit with current projects, which projects and what would make it work or fit better. You can share what you thought was positive or negative about it, and how you see it fitting into the work context. This conversation will help you both explore the tool, technique or idea a bit more and both understand it better, and provides the opportunity to contextualize it for your work environment.

This routine can happen spontaneously, following learning something new. After you learn something new, you may gather your thoughts and think about who you want to chat about it with. If you had been in a classroom for the learning, you may have chatted with others in the class immediately. With continuous learning in the workplace, you need to look for opportunities and colleagues to discuss learning with, and you may need to explain your thinking and the new idea, as they may not have been exposed to it yet.

Reward

The reward for this routine is that you have the opportunity to collaborate and innovate with colleagues, which makes work more engaging and connects you with your colleagues better. Taking the opportunity to chat about new tools and techniques with colleagues in one-on-one conversations, especially in hybrid work environments where people are working in a mixture of office and at home, can help you feel more connected. Getting into the habit of having these conversations can help you to collaborate better, especially in a fully remote environment. The conversations can spark new ideas and help you understand what you are learning better.

Context

The context that supports this habit is that you build an environment where learning is expected and shared, and you have colleagues who discuss learning and ideas together. If this isn't the context within your current network, try some of these conversations to start changing that context. And if your current network is not receptive to it, or you just want to expand the conversation, reach out to new colleagues or chat with others that you haven't had this type of conversation with before. It is a low-risk activity and can actually be used as a precursor to perhaps finding an accountability partner or even opportunities to collaborate at work in your role.

FIGURE 19.1   Conversations habit

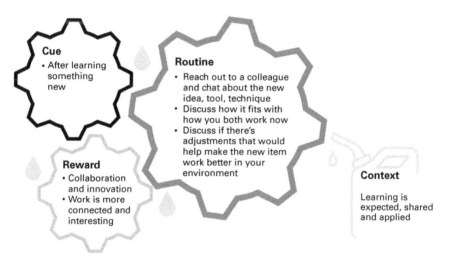

Measurement for the habit

This is a very informal habit so you can use the measurements here to decide what good looks like for you. You could informally track your progress against one or more of these areas, to keep yourself on track with using the habit.

- Number of conversations that touched on learning – per week, per month.

- Number of people you chatted with about learning ideas – this is particularly relevant if you want to grow your network.

- Number of conversations per person – this is relevant if you want to deepen your connection with particular people, perhaps moving towards an accountability partnership or mentor relationship.

- Length of conversations – do you want to have quick short conversations, or longer more in-depth conversations? Which do you like better? Does it vary by person? By topic?

- Variety of learning ideas/tools/techniques discussed – are you going to go deep on a particular topic and focus your conversations there or did you want to have a wide variety of subject areas?

- Number of conversations within your current company vs number of conversations outside of your company.

These are general metrics you can choose to use as needed. You may find it beneficial to just review the list periodically and think about your progress.

Make this habit AUTOMATIC

A – Allow for feeling good. This habit is an informal one so keep the conversations fun. Look for people you want to connect with and find opportunities to chat. You could also use learning and the ideas in this habit for something to chat about at work events, especially if finding common conversation areas is challenging.

U – Under the influence. When getting started with this habit, see if there are others who you admire who use a similar habit for conversations. You may begin to notice that some people bring up articles, books or ideas they've recently learned, in conversation – check how they do it and build on that.

T – **Tip the scale.** As you start with this habit or begin to use it more frequently, seek out others who may be using this habit and ask them about how it works for them and how they use it. You could share the idea for the habit with others on your team or in your network and chat about how it might work for you both. This type of conversation is an example of using this habit already, as you've learned about the habit and are chatting with others about how it might fit.

O – **Ownership.** As you start to use this habit, particularly if it feels a little out of character for you or uncomfortable, think to yourself that this is something you do. Think about the value of these types of conversations for both you and the person you're chatting with, and think of yourself as someone who uses this habit. It will help you begin to have ownership over the habit so you adopt it as something that you do. This also helps you to have ownership over your implementation intentions of how you'll use the new habit; you'll be viewing the world through the lens of someone who uses this habit and then actively doing it.

M – **Mindset.** As you use this habit and have conversations, a growth mindset will be key to getting the most out of your conversations. As you go into the conversations, consider that you aren't quite sure about the new idea, tool or technique yet, and you're looking to explore different perspectives on it. This type of attitude will keep you open to influence from others so you can consider their ideas, input and perspectives. If you go in with a set perspective, you may come across as just explaining the new idea, but the conversation may die there as you're not giving the appearance of looking for input or new perspectives, rather you're more in teaching mode. Stay in learning mode as you use this habit and have conversations that explore and expand on your thinking.

A – **Avoid losses.** If you're not comfortable yet with chatting with others about what you're finding and learning, then consider trying out this habit in a low-risk, safe space first. Try it out with someone you trust and you can even explain you're looking to explore the new ideas with them. Once you've tried it out with a few people you trust, you'll gain confidence to expand to chatting with others. You will find that even if some people are not interested or even disagree, you'll consider that a learning experience and a worthwhile effort, even if the conversation didn't go how you thought it might.

T – Towards the default. Attentional scarcity and time pressure are real in many organizations. If using this habit feels like yet another thing you need to schedule time for, you're considering it too formally. Just use time that occurs by default – if you're in a meeting early take a few minutes to chat ideas, if a meeting wraps up early and you have the opportunity, chat in the last few minutes.

I – Incentives. This habit provides the benefit of collaboration and innovation, and helps you better understand your learning. But it also has some immediate benefits in deepening conversations and potentially expanding your network. By using this habit, you are enriching your conversations, which will provide short-term benefits and long-term gains as you build your skills over time.

C – Commitment. To get started with this habit, have a look at the measurement suggestions above and make a commitment to yourself to get started and by how much. For example, you could commit to chatting with one person this week on one topic. Pick a starting point and commit to delivering on it.

YOUR ACTION PLAN

As you look at using this habit, or expanding on your existing use of the habit, consider the AUTOMATIC suggestions to make the habit work for you. Think about the measurements suggested so you have an idea of how much you want to use the habit. But even before both of those things, try it out.

This is an informal habit so you can be quite informal in using it. After you have come across something from your ongoing learning, think about who you can chat about it with, and then find some time to chat. This is a low-risk habit to get started, but it can be very powerful in helping you to expand your ideas, apply them and build a network to support you as you learn.

To make your action plan, formulate your cue based on how you learn – do you read daily? When are you learning and when would make sense to chat with others? Who will you chat with? Co-workers? Colleagues outside of work? Someone on your commute? Family members? Then when you are chatting find a routine that works for you – the conversation will vary depending on who you are chatting with but remember the mindset – be open and flexible in your thinking to gather insight from your conversations. And then consider what the rewards are for you – periodically reflect on your use of the habit to consider how it is benefitting you. It is a simple habit, but the benefits build up over time, so it is good to look back periodically and recognize how it has helped you. Finally, if your current context doesn't support the use of this habit, expand your network and find people that will be open to these types of conversations.

Back to our story

At that technical team that we heard about at the beginning of the chapter, with the great collaboration and ongoing conversations, they have had several members move on from the team. Technical folks often move around as their skills are in high demand. But something was different about this team, a disproportionate number of the team members went on to leadership roles, either within the same company or at new companies. The sharing and collaboration on the team not only helped the team achieve their results together as a team, it helped the team members build their skills and go on to lead successful careers in technology.

The cross-pollination of ideas through conversation is a powerful component that can help you learn and synthesize new ideas and help you be more successful and make your work more interesting. Being on a team that does this can make work more enjoyable and help everyone be more successful. Think about how you can begin or expand your use of conversations after learning.

Key takeaways

- The conversation habit is an informal one, it can help you better understand your learning, apply new ideas and expand your network and collaboration.

• The conversation habit can help you build your network and can lead to finding an accountability partner or mentor.

TABLE 19.1 Make the conversations habit AUTOMATIC

AUTOMATIC	Conversations habit ....
Allow for feeling good To get it done, make it fun.	Keep the conversation casual and look for opportunities where it might fit with people who would be good to chat with.
Under the influence If the leader is a gem, we'll follow them.	Seek out people you admire who already use this habit effectively and learn from their approach.
Tip the scale If we can't see it, we often won't do it.	Ask others how they discuss new learning and what works for them.
Ownership If it's mine, I think it's super fine.	Consider conversations about learning items as something that you do to help you understand and socialize new ideas.
Mindset As a skill set grows, our fixed mindset will decompose.	As you chat about new ideas, consider different points of view and if you need to adjust your thinking.
Avoid losses Don't ignore a potential gain just because a loss would be a pain.	If chatting about new learning ideas is unfamiliar, and feels uncomfortable, consider trying it with someone you trust first.
Towards the default To be quick, go with the default pick.	Try chatting at the beginning or ends of meetings, to use time already in your calendar, with co-workers.
Incentives A bird in the hand is worth two in the bush.	Consider the benefit of expanding your conversations and network.
Commitment If I say it, I better do it.	To get started, commit to chatting with one person, once a week, about new ideas or learning.

PART FIVE

Bringing it all together

20

Bringing it all together

Since I started writing this book in 2021, we've seen inflation skyrocket, interest rates rise, gas prices increase to unprecedented levels and war in Europe. These events caught many people by surprise; even recognized experts did not anticipate the changes we've seen. We cannot predict the future, but we can prepare ourselves to be as ready as possible.

In this book I've shared tools to help you understand the importance of habits, to see a way of measuring habits for your organization through the LEARN model and an anatomy of a habit to help you break down activities to ensure a cue, routine, reward and supporting context. We've looked at ways to make each habit AUTOMATIC, discussed measurement and suggested ways to build an action plan for each habit.

As you put together your action plan, you need the right resources available. For those responsible for learning and development in the organization, and who are looking to move to support a continuous learning environment, let's look now at the resources or roles to support learning habits.

Defining roles

Through these definitions of roles for building a learning culture, you can recognize your role and the role of others in your organization.

For each role, I'll explain what they are responsible for with learning habits, what skills they need and which activities they support. In the additional resources section, I'll share a dashboard tool that you can use to determine the capabilities you currently have access to and which ones you need to foster or build within your organization. You may have these roles in your organization, but they may not yet focus or be responsible for learning habits. The roles described here exist today in many companies. Added here you'll find how they would tie to learning habits when using the approach in this book.

Executive guidance

The first type of role is at the executive level. We'll refer to this type of role collectively as executive guidance, and we'll focus specifically on executives involved in driving organizational learning:

Sample job titles:

- VP Learning, Chief Learning Officer, Chief Human Resources Officer, SVP Learning and Talent

Responsibilities:

- ensures learning habits are aligned to key performance indicators in support of corporate strategy
- manages the overall strategic learning culture and habits
- models the behaviour and sets the expectations around learning habits
- socializes learning habits at executive level

Skills needed:

- a strong understanding of key performance indicators and organizational initiatives
- innovative leader who fosters strong communication

Activities they support:

- building executive buy in for learning habits

Programme management

Programme management is anyone responsible for an organizational learning strategy, learning programme or multiple learning programmes in an organization.

Sample job titles:

- AVP Learning, Senior Manager Learning, Learning Manager

Responsibilities:

- executes deployment of learning habits in line with strategic plan for learning culture and habits
- liaison across the business to ensure ongoing effectiveness, business alignment and resources for learning culture and habits
- review and communicates results, adjusts and update plans

Skills needed:

- effective vision, leadership and resource management skills, and the ability to keep teams and learning habits on target

Activities they support:

- general oversight and tracking against overall learning habits plans across all teams

Administration

Administration is anyone responsible for the logistics of a learning programme or the administration of a learning system online.

Sample job titles:

- Human Resources Administrator, Data and Analytics lead for HR, LMS Administrator, HR Operations Analyst

Responsibilities:

- report on metrics and results in line with learning habits measurement

- liaison with business units to get metrics aligned with learning habits measurement

Skills needed:

- excellent organizational skills as well as proficiency with spreadsheets and data visualizations
- understanding of metrics and key performance indicators for reporting purposes

Activities they support:

- enabling programme management to share results of learning habits via appropriate data and visualizations

Communications

Communications is anyone involved in corporate communications, and also those involved in learning communications or human resources communications.

Sample job titles:

- Corporate Communications Manager, Learning Communications Manager, HR Communications

Responsibilities:

- design and manage strategic communications plan and aligned assets in support of learning culture and learning habits strategy

Skills needed:

- strong marketing, communication and messaging skills
- strong understanding of effective communication methods within the specific audience and organization context

Activities they support:

- enabling executive guidance and programme management in ongoing communication for learning habits and learning culture

Line of business executive

Next we have the line of business executive. This refers to leadership within lines of business in an organization, as opposed to the executive guidance we looked at earlier that is for learning specifically.
  Sample job titles:

- line of business leadership titles such as Vice President of Information Technology and any director level and above leader for any group outside of learning or human resources

Responsibilities:

- share line of business key performance indicators to ensure team can align learning habits plan to effectively impact the business
- set the expectation and model the behaviour of learning habits for their business unit

Skills needed:

- understand and communicate key performance indicators
- ability to help corporate team align learning habits effectively to key performance indicators

Activities they support:

- enabling the corporate learning culture strategy and learning habits within their business unit

Manager

The sixth type of role is the manager role. This refers collectively to all people leaders across all lines of business within a company.
  Job titles:

- all people leader titles across the business

Responsibilities:

- sets the expectation and models the behaviour for learning habits and learning culture in line with corporate strategy

Skills needed:

- ability to see how learning habits can support the results the team needs to achieve
- ability to understand that learning is an important but not urgent item and still needs to have time allocated for it
- ability to act on supporting learning habits by communication and time allocation

Activities they support:

- enabling the team's development and learning habits

Individual contributor

Finally, we have individual contributors. This refers to all those within the company who do not have people reporting to them, making them individual contributors.

Job titles:

- any individual contributor title – anyone in the business that does not have people reporting to them

Responsibilities:

- understands the expectations and models the behaviour for learning habits to support a learning culture in the organization

Skills needed:

- ability to see how learning habits can support the results they need to achieve and how to apply them in the context of their work

Activities they support:

- helps peers' development and learning habits

Your next steps

Now that you have the tools to understand a learning culture through the lens of learning habits, you can see where your organization is currently with the LEARN model, you can build a plan for each habit that you would like to have used, decide how to measure each habit, make them AUTOMATIC and ensure that your roles are aligned to your learning habit strategy.

I mentioned at the beginning of the book that learning habits are like exercise, you don't get in shape and then stop working out, it's a continual process. I'd like to leave you with another metaphor. To help our organizations ensure learning habits are AUTOMATIC, it is like driving a vehicle. To move forward you need to put your foot on the accelerator. There may be times when you can coast down a hill, but it takes constant steering and acceleration along the journey. Think of the LEARN model as your GPS to decide on your destination, and think of AUTOMATIC and your learning habits plans as the fuel to get you there. I wish you all the best on your journey – it is an interesting and worthwhile ride!

21

Additional resources

To implement the ideas in this book, it can help to have some tools and templates. Here are resources to help assess the roles in your organization as well as an overview of resources available online based on the contents of the book.

Assessment of roles in your organization

To identify your next step in supporting learning habits, review the role descriptions below and mark if you have that role in place, then mark the level of depth in that role and finally, note who is currently in that role.

Role identification

TABLE 21.1 Role details and identification

Role	Sample titles	Responsibilities	Skills needed	Supports	Role filled?
Executive guidance	VP Learning, Chief Learning Officer, Chief Human Resources Officer, SVP Learning and Talent.	Ensures learning habits are aligned to key performance indicators in support of corporate strategy. Manages the overall strategic learning culture and habits. Models the behaviour and sets the expectations around learning habits. Socializes learning habits at executive level.	A strong understanding of key performance indicators and organizational initiatives. Innovative leader who fosters strong communication.	Building executive buy in for learning habits.	
Programme management	AVP Learning, Senior Manager Learning, Learning Manager.	Executes deployment of learning habits in line with strategic plan for learning culture and habits. Liaison across the business to ensure ongoing effectiveness, business alignment and resources for learning culture and habits. Review and communicates results, adjusts and update plans.	Effective vision, leadership and resource management skills and the ability to keep teams and learning habits on target.	General oversight and tracking against overall learning habits plans across all teams.	

(continued)

TABLE 21.1 (Continued)

Role	Sample titles	Responsibilities	Skills needed	Supports	Role filled?
Administration	Human Resources Administrator Data and Analytics lead for HR, LMS Administrator, HR Operations Analyst.	Report on metrics and results in line with learning habits measurement. Liaison with business units to get metrics aligned with learning habits measurement.	Excellent organizational skills as well as proficiency with spreadsheets and data visualizations. Understanding of metrics and key performance indicators for reporting purposes.	Enabling programme management to share results of learning habits via appropriate data and visualizations.	
Communications	Corporate Communications Manager, Learning Communications Manager, HR Communications.	Design and manage strategic communications plan and aligned assets in support of learning culture and learning habits strategy.	Strong marketing, communication and messaging skills. Strong understanding of effective communication methods within the specific audience and organization context.	Enabling executive guidance and programme management in ongoing communication for learning habits and learning culture.	

Line of business executives	Line of business leadership titles such as Vice President of Information Technology and any Director level and above leader for any group outside of learning or human resources.	Share line of business key performance indicators to ensure team can align learning habits plan to effectively impact the business. Set the expectation and model the behaviour of learning habits for their business unit.	Understand and communicate key performance indicators. Ability to help corporate team align learning habits effectively to key performance indicators.	Enabling the corporate learning culture strategy and learning habits within their business unit.
Manager	All people leader titles across the business.	Sets the expectation and models the behaviour for learning habits and learning culture in line with corporate strategy.	Ability to see how learning habits can support the results the team needs to achieve. Ability to understand that learning is an important but not urgent item and still needs to have time allocated for it. Ability to act on supporting learning habits by communication and time allocation.	Enabling the team's development and learning habits.
Individual contributor	Any individual contributor title – anyone in the business that does not have people reporting to them.	Understands the expectations and models the behaviour for learning habits to support a learning culture in the organization.	Ability to see how learning habits can support the results they need to achieve and how to apply them in the context of their work.	Helps peers' development and learning habits.

Roles: Current depth

Use Table 21.2 to rate your current depth of support for learning habits across each role area. If you do not have anyone for the particular area, mark that as none and determine a plan to identify who would fit that role. Keep in mind that you may have a person who does more than one role.

TABLE 21.2 Assessing current depth

Role	None	Poor	Fair	Good	Exceptional	Next step
Executive guidance						
Programme management						
Administration						
Communications						
Line of business executives						
Manager						
Individual contributor						

Roles: Directory

Use Table 21.3 to identify who is currently in the roles. Keep in mind that you may have a person that is in more than one role. If you do not have someone in the particular role area, identify your next step to move someone into that role.

TABLE 21.3 Identifying current resources

Capability	Name	Name	Name	Name	Name
Executive guidance					
Programme management					
Administration					
Communications					
Line of business executives					
Manager					
Individual contributor					

Resource: Habit slides

Access the Kogan Page website for slides based on the habit graphics shared in the chapters. You can then tweak them for your audience and share.

Resource: Make habits AUTOMATIC

Find downloadable versions of the AUTOMATIC table and each of the versions for each habit at the Kogan Page website.

Resource: AIM to LEARN discussion slides

Download a set of slides that you can customize and use to support your meetings with stakeholders in the Align phase of AIM.

Check out the Kogan Page site for resources and visit my website at www.yoursuccesspartnernow.com for updates as I research and build more materials.

INDEX

Note: Page numbers in *italics* refer to tables or figures

CPSIA information can be obtained
at www.ICGtesting.com
Printed in the USA
JSHW041439240323
39427JS00007B/37